Secrets in the Genes

Adoption, inheritance and genetic disease

Edited by Peter Turnpenny

with Donal Giltinan
        Anne Grant
        Michael Morton

B *r i t i s h*

A *g e n c i e s*

f o r **A** *d o p t i o n*

a n d **F** *o s t e r i n g*

Published by
British Agencies for Adoption & Fostering
(BAAF)
Skyline House
200 Union Street
London SE1 0LX
Registered Charity 275689

© BAAF 1995

**British Library Cataloguing in Publication
Data**
Secrets in the Genes:
Adoption, inheritance and genetic disease
    I. Turnpenny, Peter
    362.734

    ISBN 1-873868-16-2

Designed by Andrew Haig & Associates
Typeset, printed and bound by Russell Press
(TU) in Great Britain

Contents

Foreword

Donal Giltinan

In Plato's Dialogue, *The Apology*, Socrates makes the astounding statement that the unexamined life is not worth living. Nowhere is life, in all its dimensions, examined more closely than in the processes of adoption, fostering and child care in general. The lives of children and their families, old and new, are microscopically scrutinised in an attempt to understand human behaviour and achieve wellbeing.

The science of human genetics traces its origins to the publication in 1869 of *Hereditary Genius*, a book by Darwin's cousin, Francis Galton. The early history of this science is somewhat chequered but the rapid advances of the last twenty five years have made an invaluable contribution to our understanding of the influence of nature and nurture on human development. In 1980 BAAF published a small booklet called *Genetics in Adoption and Fostering* which was based on Professor Cedric Carter's Hilda Lewis Memorial Lecture of the previous year. Practitioners in the field of adoption and fostering found this booklet enormously helpful but in the intervening fifteen years there has been very rapid growth in our understanding of genetics.

The aim of this book is to inform child care workers of all disciplines about some aspects of genetics with a view to enhancing the lives of the children and young people that they work for and with.

This is not a definitive book; difficult choices had to be made about what to include and what to consign to 'further relevant reading' for the interested reader to pursue. There are many new areas to explore and further developments still to come. The authors provide basic background information and attempt to address common questions that arise for workers who are professionally involved in adoption and fostering but who are 'lay persons' in the field of genetics. They also lead the reader through the moral maze of issues such as confidentiality, disclosure and non-disclosure, pausing at some of the questions and veiling many of the answers with a caveat of 'it all depends'.

It is the intention of the authors to provide the readers with knowledge rather than answers. As well as providing basic information some of the chapters provide very specific and sometimes technical information on particular topics. While these may be relevant to parents and social workers they will be of particular interest to medical advisers and clinicians in the child care field. The chapters on psychiatric, learning and behaviour disorders, cancer genetics, congenital heart disease, cardiovascular disease and diabetes, as well as the chapter on the future of genetics in medicine and society, all fall into this category.

There will be few readers who will want to read this book from cover to cover. It is more a compendium of articles around the particular theme of genetics in adoption and fostering and the reader is more likely to select chapters that are relevant to a specific situation.

This book is the result of the hard work of many people. First the members of the committee of the Scottish Medical Group of BAAF who responded enthusiastically to a suggestion first put forward by Dr Eugenia Ngwane that such a book was necessary and to Dr Peter Turnpenny himself whose persistence and patience elicited contributions from some of the most informed people on this subject.

This exploration will undoubtedly unveil answers to questions about our genetic histories but each answer will also bring with it further questions about the ethics and morality of how we use our new knowledge.

Introduction

Dr Peter Turnpenny

We share our genes with our biological relatives. This obvious and non-controversial fact barely needs stating in an age when so many of the fundamental processes that govern and drive nature are well understood and yielding their secrets almost daily to the power of modern scientific investigation. Yet this is a profound reality too, for our genetic make-up is one of the most basic and important common denominators shared with other family members. Genes, to a very large extent, determine our physical characteristics, intellect, behaviour, and predisposition to illness and disease. They are, however, not the only influence, particularly on behaviour, intellect and personality. Debate has long raged about the relative contributions of nature and nurture that determine individual character and achievement. Humankind is manifestly more than a functional biological species and generally lives in sophisticated social structures which seek to maintain moral standards and ethical values. In many areas of human concern, therefore, the biological and social sciences are convergent and intertwined. It is the task of this book to explore the interface between these sciences in one area of concern, namely the adoption process.

Recent advances in genetic technology, sometimes called 'the new genetics', make it possible to study human identity in a novel way by analysing the chemical of inheritance, DNA (deoxyribonucleic acid). Patterns of DNA structure, including those associated with disease genes, can be tracked through families with relative ease, making it possible to know which 'markers' and/or genes we have in common with our children, parents, siblings, and members of the wider family. It is appreciated that new ethical dilemmas have arisen as a consequence, such as the sharing of genetic information[1,2,3] and the possibility of presymptomatic screening for serious disease(s) with no satisfactory treatment. These issues, together with new options for choice in the field

1

of reproductive medicine created by advances in molecular and cell biology, as well as the potential for genetic engineering, have fired the imagination of both the media and the public. Such interest has spawned a plethora of popular articles and books, besides television and radio programmes, for the consumer public, some of which, it must be said, have been far more sensational than sensible. The public, however, are generally aware that a biotechnological revolution is underway and many are inquisitive, wondering where it will all lead and what it might be able to offer.

On the other hand, much research has been conducted into the nature of identity formation in adopted people, seeking to unravel the reasons why a significant proportion embark on a search of their origins.[4,5,6] These are complex issues for which we do not have clear and simple answers. We can talk vaguely of multiple psychological and socio-cultural influences which contribute to identity formation but underneath, as it were, genetically determined controls are at work, probably exercising a remarkable degree of flexibility to allow adaptation to change. The more we learn about the developing brain, the more we should marvel at its amazing complexity of function at a very early age. Research in this area, towards understanding the mechanisms of behavioural imprinting through the mother–infant bonding relationship, or alternatively through the stranger–infant relationship, has direct relevance for adoption and identity formation, in particular, the placement of emotionally disturbed children following neglect or abuse.

Clients attending genetic clinics often ask searching questions about matters relevant to them; it should not be surprising, therefore, if adopted adults, prospective adoptive parents, and birth parents, ask equally searching questions about inheritance and genetic disease as it applies to their particular situation. Those working at the coal face of adoption practice should therefore be trying to stay one step ahead, anticipating the issues and knowing when and how to seek help if necessary. Those adopted people who embark on a search do so to fill a vacuum in their lives that cannot be satisfied in any other way. They generally want to know what their genetic parents are like, both physically and as personalities, and whether they are healthy. This may come into sharp focus when the adopted person faces childbearing and rearing themselves or, as I have witnessed in the genetic clinic, when they become the parent of a child with a defect. What is not known with any accuracy is the actual proportion of adopted people for whom the search becomes a burning issue and the real underlying reasons why the vacuum exists at all. To what extent are genetic factors per se responsible for the impulses which drive many to seek links with their genetic lineage and social origins in order to fill the identity gap? The answer is not known but it is a legitimate question.

As a clinical geneticist, my own interest in adoption was aroused by cases where an inherited disease emerged in a birth parent some years after the child was placed. The nature of the disease(s) had important health implications for the long separated child *if* it had inherited the gene fault. However, there was no protocol in place for dealing with the problem of how and when the information should reach the child. The legal guidelines, it appeared, could be interpreted to provide authority for an adoption agency to communicate to an adopted child, or the adoptive parents, medical information concerning the birth parents where to do so would be in accordance with the needs and interests of the child. For some this might be considered adequate, since each adoption situation is unique, but experience in the genetic clinic shows that disclosure of information within 'normal' families is sometimes sensitive and contentious. My colleagues and I were therefore not satisfied that the problems of inherited disease within the adoption circle lacked a profile of their own. With the advent of genetic testing and screening by DNA analysis we began to see further important issues which needed to be addressed in adoption. This book, to a very real extent, is a part of an ongoing process to raise awareness of the potential importance and application of new genetic technology in this field.

At a relatively early stage in our quest to find out more it became apparent that we were only rediscovering what many medical advisers and social workers were already familiar with in their own practice, namely, that difficult and sensitive situations concerning family medical history and confidentiality do occur. That a genetic disease might manifest itself after the placement of the child, perhaps years later, should not be surprising. It is not generally well apppreciated that diseases which have at least some hereditary component to their aetiology (cause) are common. In a large survey in British Columbia, Canada, Baird et al demonstrated that at least five per cent of the population showed signs of a condition with a genetic factor by the age of 25, and this excluded severe malformations that were lethal in early childhood.[7] By the age of 60 this figure had risen to 60 per cent when many of the common disorders, which also have a genetic component, such as cardiovascular and autoimmune diseases, as well as cancer, were included. Whilst a large proportion of all these are not 'single gene' conditions with a simple pattern of inheritance carrying a high recurrence risk, they are nevertheless the subject of intense genetic research which will, more and more, arouse the interest of the general public as breakthroughs are made. Therefore, when adopted people want to know something of their birth parents' medical histories, how much will it be possible to provide in an age when this information may increasingly be seen as directly relevant to personal health? Of course, with increasing openness in adoption some of these problems are likely to diminish but retrospectively there are still vast numbers of adopted people for whom the information would be difficult, if not impossible, to obtain if they sought it. In England and Wales 879,601 adoptions were registered from 1927-90, and in Scotland 84,428 from 1931-90[8] (adoption was given legal status in England and Wales in 1926 and in Scotland in 1930).

Advances in genetics therefore raise a number of new issues which need special consideration within the context of adoption. There are aspects which concern all three parties. Firstly, the adopted people themselves, for whom the question of precise diagnosis and possible genetic tests pertaining to birth parents and other biological relatives is potentially of great importance to them. Secondly, adoptive parents, because they will take on legal responsibility for a child, may request both detailed medical information about the birth parents and certain genetic tests, which are not routinely performed, to be carried out on the child. Furthermore, there is an obligation on adoption agencies to ensure that the adoptive parents will be able to look after children throughout childhood and this raises questions about their own risk of genetic disease which might be a compromising factor. Thirdly, birth parents and their biological relatives may expect to have the opportunity, for instance for carrier testing, in the event that the adopted person develops a genetic disease such as cystic fibrosis or Fragile X syndrome. The critical issues to be addressed, therefore, are the following.

1) Who owns our genetic information?

Clearly, as individuals, we have a right to medical confidentiality but do biological relatives not have a right also to information which may directly affect their health and reproductive decisions? If consent is given to disclose information, as it very often is, then the issue is whether the unsuspecting person will be grateful for that information or prefer to remain ignorant. If consent for disclosure is not obtained there must be a judgement as to whether the individual's right to confidentiality can be legitimately overridden. It is increasingly recognised that such difficult circumstances occasionally occur[9] but within the adoption circle confidentiality issues are even more complex and need special consideration.

2) Family medical history sought prior to the placement

For infants given up for adoption there are often great difficulties experienced in obtaining detailed information about the child's father and grandparents. This is a stressful time for the birth mother and she may not be very forthcoming. In addition, much of the questioning is carried out by social workers with no medical training. Increasingly, as more becomes possible in the field of medical genetics, attention to detail is vital if accurate information is to be passed on to adoptive parents. Often the information will not be complete, and it may not be possible to initiate further investigations of the birth mother's parents, for instance, because of confidentialty problems.

3) Screening for genetic disease

There is much interest in what might become feasible in screening all newborns beyond what is currently practised. However, if there is no treatment for a disorder for which a screening test is possible, there are ethical questions about whether the test should be done. If it can help prevent the birth of a second affected baby, however, then some would consider the policy justified; this has been proposed for the sex-linked condition Duchenne muscular dystrophy.[10] The question here is whether infants and children for adoption should be the subject of a different policy on screening from that of the general population. If so, would this jeopardise the chance of an early placement for the infant, and would it remove the adopted person's choice to be tested in later life? It should be borne in mind that screening may have implications in areas of social importance, such as employment and life insurance.

4) Storage of DNA
DNA can be easily extracted from a blood sample and stored indefinitely at low temperatures. If the birth parents/mother consented to having a sample stored at the time when the child is adopted, genetic information might be made available at a later stage for the benefit of the adopted person, if appropriate. This would avoid some of the potential difficulties relating to confidentiality and tracing, but mechanisms for registering the storage would have to be established and access to the sample protected.

5) Tracing of individuals and medical records
Sometimes accurate information is only possible when key individuals in a biological family and/or their records can be traced. However, any proposals that make it easier to find people are likely to be unacceptable and raise further questions about confidentiality.

In this introduction I have sought to raise the issues and pose some of the questions from the standpoint of clinical genetics. Professionals in the field of adoption may see the issues from other perspectives with different emphases. It is therefore important that this book reflects the viewpoints of different disciplines. This collection contains articles by individuals with a special interest or expertise. Taken together it is hoped they form a coherent whole and will address many pertinent issues for those for whom it is intended, namely social workers, medical advisers and any others with an interest in the adoption process. The collection has been divided into three sections, each of which is introduced. Section 1 explores the role of genetics in the adoption process; Section 2 provides the genetic basis of hereditary disease and an overview of some medical applications; Section 3 discusses genetic testing and screening and the ethical issues that arise when considering the sharing of that information.

The book begins by discussing a representative set of questions which are among those uppermost in the minds of adoption workers and prospective adoptive parents. Many do not have straightforward answers and, as far as the science of medical genetics is concerned, it is obviously not possible to speculate beyond the limits of current knowledge but some are specifically addressed in later sections. We have tried to provide a simplified scientific update from both laboratory and clinical perspectives but have not attempted to make this a comprehensive textbook of medical genetics. For many genetic diseases the interested reader will have to look elsewhere but in highlighting psychiatric and behavioural disorders, cancer, and cardiovascular disease, we have hopefully given consideration to areas which are both relevant and difficult in the context of adoption. They also serve to illustrate the rapid scientific advance that is underway. We have included an important contribution from another growth area of research, namely the psychosocial aspects of genetic testing and counselling. Recently the Clinical Genetics Society of the UK produced a working party report on the genetic testing of children, a document with obvious relevance to adoption, and this has been helpfully summarised. We have also tried to look into the future and the book concludes with contributions from genetic science and, finally, the implications for adoption work in a changing world. As such, it is hoped that this will be a useful aid and resource to those who face these issues in their daily work.

Having had the task of co-ordinating this compilation, I must express my thanks to the many authors who have contributed so willingly and enthusiastically, a response which has made the process both an encouragement and a pleasure.

References

1   Richards J R, Bobrow M, 'Ethical issues in clinical genetics', *Journal of the Royal College of Physicians*, 25:284-88, 1991.

2   *Report of the Committee on the Ethics of Gene Therapy*, January 1992: 15-16, HMSO.

3   Nuffield Council on Bioethics, *Genetic screening: ethical issues*, 41-53, December 1993.

4   McWhinnie A M, *Adopted Children: How they grow up*, Routledge & Kegan Paul, 1967.

5   Triseliotis J, *In Search of Origins*, Routledge & Kegan Paul, 1973.

6   *The Psychology of Adoption*, eds. Brodzinsky D M, Schechter M D, Oxford University Press, 1990.

7   Baird P A, Anderson T W, Newcombe H B, Lowry R B, 'Genetic disorders in children and young adults: a population study', *American Journal of Human Genetics*, 42:677-93, 1988, USA.

8   Registrar General for Scotland, *Annual report of the Registrar General for Scotland 1990*, General Register Office, Edinburgh 142, 1991.

9   See 3 above.

10 Bradley D M, Parsons E P, Clarke A J, 'Experience with screening newborns for Duchenne muscular dystrophy in Wales', *British Medical Journal*, 306:357-60, 1993.

Section 1
Genetics and the adoption process

While this book will have a significant academic component in discussing the relevance of modern medical genetics to adoption, it is vital that the situations and complexities of real life lie at its heart. In this opening section, therefore, the experiences of professionals in relation to heredity and genetic disease are discussed from different points of view (Chapters 1 – 4). Medical advisers, in their assessment of a particular case, will inevitably focus on the technical aspects of a disease or disorder – the precise diagnosis, the aetiology, the prognosis, the need for further investigation and ongoing surveillance, and its medical relevance for the other parties of the adoption circle. Social workers, however, will be particularly concerned with the human and relational impact of a medical condition – the implications with respect to social needs and coping mechanisms for the adopted individual and the adoptive family, as well as birth parents and their families. Those who work in the field, regardless of their professional discipline, will be able to identify with much of what is presented in this section and may well have come across cases similar to, and perhaps even more striking than, the consecutive series described in Chapter 4.

The last contribution in this section, Chapter 5, is intended to provide a bridge with Section 2. Past studies on adopted individuals and their families have been important in highlighting the genetic component of a variety of medical conditions, mostly in relation to mental health but also in other areas. This short chapter acknowledges that contribution and mentions the large ongoing longitudinal studies from which further data on the heritability of many aspects of behaviour and personality may eventually emerge.

1 Common questions that arise at adoption

Dr Michael Morton and Dr Margaret Irving

When a child is being adopted, parents and professionals commonly raise certain questions which have a direct bearing on inherited characteristics and hereditary disease. In this chapter, the authors draw upon their own experience and that of their colleagues, to introduce these questions and begin to address them. Many of the issues raised in this chapter are discussed in detail elsewhere in this collection.

What sort of person will this be?

When a child is being placed for adoption one of the most pressing questions is always:

Will the child be healthy?

Around three to four per cent of newborn babies go on to develop disability in childhood and there can be no guarantee of health. Indications of outcome which may be reassuring can be drawn from the child's current state of health and appearance at examination and in most cases no elaborate medical testing is required. A good family history will add significantly to the chances of accurate prediction. Social workers should know the importance of establishing as much as possible of the background of the child and his or her family including both physical and mental diseases. Such information may provide a key to understanding the health needs of a child after adoption, but there is always a need for professionals and families to learn to live with uncertainty.

When a baby is born, much is made of family resemblance; it is not surprising to hear questions on this subject in baby adoption.

How much is physical appearance determined by genes?

Some aspects of appearance may be predictable; transmission of hair colour varies according to the genetic make up of parents, for example, red hair is a genetically determined characteristic and may appear with two black haired parents. Height can generally be predicted by mean parental height but there is considerable variability. Prediction depends on knowing physical details of both birth parents. Sometimes in baby adoption it may be felt to be important to consider such factors for matching, although more emphasis is placed on other qualities. The issue of matching for appearance is discussed further in Chapter 2.

One of the more controversial questions concerns:
The role of genetic factors in the development of intelligence
Certain genetically determined syndromes have a relatively predictable effect on intelligence but even in such cases there can be considerable variation, for example, individuals with Down's syndrome (a chromoso-mal abnormality) may have moderately severe mental retardation at one end of the spectrum, or may occasionally have only mild learning difficulties. Such variability makes prediction in individual cases a hazardous affair. There is controversy about suggestions that parental intellectual level predicts child outcome through genetic mechanisms (in the absence of well defined syndromes). It is likely that intellectual ability is in part determined by constitutional factors transmitted through multiple genetic influences but this may not outweigh the importance of early environment for intellectual development. When children are placed after prolonged periods of social, emotional and even nutritional privation, these environmental factors may be more important than genetic influences. Intelligence alone does not predict later attainment as other factors are of equal or greater importance.

The main focus of genetic research has been on matters of medical concern. Such research gives little guidance in answering another question that is commonly raised:
Will the child be musical/artistic?
In cases where a child comes from a family with a strong history of musical or artistic achievement there is a possibility that a child may share traits with birth family members that could predispose the child to similar interests. Life history may be as important as genetics and it may be helpful to find a positive link with the child's past through artistic

interests, although too high an expectation may lead to the opposite effect with the child rejecting art or music.

The genetic importance of the social background history
Although race and heredity can make an inflammable mixture, there are some established facts to consider in response to the following question: *Are there special inherited conditions that may be predicted according to the ethnic origin of a child?*

This question is discussed in more detail in Chapter 12. An example of an autosomal recessive disorder of this kind is thalassaemia, an anaemic blood discorder (haemoglobinopathy) associated with sple-nomegaly which is a problem more likely to be found in children of Mediterranean origin. Other important recessive conditions are Tay-Sachs disease which occurs more frequently in Ashkenazi Jews and sickle cell anaemia in African-Caribbean communities. When there is a possibility of such a disorder, specialist advice may be required. Other concerns about ethnicity and genetic disease may be more speculative and value laden. For example, some psychiatric literature contains suggestions that certain ethnic groups may be more susceptible to psychotic disturbance and it is proposed that this may be due to multiple genetic factors but other experts argue that this supposed susceptibility is a result of racism. This hotly disputed issue is an example of the sensitivity of racial issues.[1] Great caution is required therefore before making predictions with regard to the relationship of ethnicity and genetics.

It is often difficult to be sure how much to push for sensitive information from a mother who is giving up her child for adoption. The social worker is right to ask:
How important is it to establish paternity?

Without reliable knowledge of paternity, it is impossible to make definitive statements on the risk of a wide range of genetic disorders, particularly those recessive conditions which only manifest when a defective gene is passed from *both* parents. There are many reasons why accurate information regarding paternity might not be available but this issue should be addressed in each case. Given developing technology genetic testing to establish paternity might be considered in some circumstances.

How important is incest?

This question relates to the frequency of genetic disease and also to major cultural taboos. Counselling of adopters should take account of potential genetic risks although these should not be over-emphasised. Consanguinity increases the incidence of abnormality since there is a greater likelihood of the same recessive gene being present in genetic material from both parents. In many cases physical disorders are not present but resultant social and emotional issues still require to be discussed with adoptive parents and possibly also with the child in later life.[2]

The importance of heredity in predicting disorder

In the face of the complex issues arising with developing genetic understanding it is legitimate to ask:

What is the use of knowing genetic predispositions?

It is increasingly possible to identify children who are at risk of developing a wide variety of physical and psychological disorders. In some cases early intervention can modify the course of the disorder, in other cases the principal concern is to ensure that prospective adoptive parents should be able to sustain their commitment in the face of predictable problems. For some families the added burden of genetic disorder may lead to difficulties and it is certainly in the best interests of the child to ensure that they are placed in a family that can cope. Biological parents and their children will understand more of the child's heredity on the basis of shared family experience than is possible in the adoptive family. The child's developing identity and the parents' coping may be greatly enhanced if the possibility of genetic disorder is understood from an early stage.

What is fixed by genes and what can be changed?

This question raises the problem of disentangling heredity and environment. Although the understanding of genetics has greatly advanced, the interaction of genetic constitution and environmental factors has by no means been understood, particularly with the more complex disorders and their effects on adjustment. Some individuals may have a constitutional vulnerability but in others resilience may also be partly constitutionally determined. Many children seeking placement will be more vulnerable because of difficulties in their early environment and this may exacerbate the effects of genetic predisposition. Of course, there are some features of an individual that are almost entirely genetically determined but even such a relatively simple item as hair colour can be altered by environmental factors and hair dye!

There is a centuries old controversy over the question:
Is anti-social behaviour purely environmental in origin?

Until recently it has often been assumed that behavioural difficulties of adopted children are due to early privation but this is not a reliable assumption. There is some evidence for a specific association between disturbed behaviour and certain defined genetic conditions such as Fragile-X syndrome, although this does not imply that behaviour disorder is inevitably found as part of this syndrome (see Chapter 8). In addition, there are aspects of the individual such as temperament which may predispose some children to behaviour disorder and such traits may be partly determined by genetic factors. Environmental factors are important causes of behaviour disorders but it is not helpful to assume that such factors are the sole reason for a child's difficulties. Failure to recognise constitutional differences between children can lead to inappropriate handling and may lead to decisions about the use of therapeutic approaches which do not adequately consider the individual needs of the child.

In view of the circumstances that may lead to a child being presented for adoption professionals are often asked the following:
What are the implications of a family history of learning difficulties or of epilepsy or of psychiatric disorder?

Some might suggest that such a family history will predispose a child to further disorder in a non specific way but this is an extremely controversial view. It is generally accepted that hereditary influences are specific to each diagnosis (see Chapter 8). Unfortunately, disorders are often not precisely diagnosed in the family history. It is not unusual for an individual to carry a variety of labels, for example, depression, alcoholism and "fits", each of which may have different hereditary implications.

Prediction in the individual case is generally not possible although for children with well established family histories of clear-cut major psychiatric disorder, it may be appropriate to comment on the risk of disorder in adulthood. It may be more important that the beliefs of potential adopters concerning the implications of a family history of mental disorder should be explored in relation to their implications for a child once adopted. Professional caution concerning prediction may reflect attitudes different from those current in the community.

Concern about future disorder may lead to the question:
What are the hereditary implications for the adopted/fostered child's own children if they have a physical disease that runs in families?

Asthma, eczema, congenital dislocation of the hip, diabetes mellitus, epilepsy, cleft lip and palate are examples of common conditions that are recognised as likely to be caused by multiple gene involvement together with environmental factors rather than by single genes. Research into such conditions continues and expert advice should be sought when an adopted person is thinking about having children. This is a situation where careful recording of genetic information prior to adoption may be of special importance in later years.

Testing issues
When a medical adviser sees a child they may be asked the following:
What tests have been done to rule out hereditary disorders?

It is important to remember that a basic medical history and physical examination will exclude many disorders. The Guthrie blood test carried out within a few days of birth will exclude two inherited conditions which can lead to permanent brain damage. In these conditions, very early diagnosis enables interventions which allow the child's normal mental development (see Chapter 12). A strong family history of any disorder may be an indication for specialist referral if not already undertaken and the medical adviser will need to explore this area.

In addition to basic medical assessment specific testing may be considered in some cases.

What tests can be done to show if a child may have hereditary problems?

Some diseases, such as diabetes mellitus, may be precipitated by environmental factors but show a statistically significant increased incidence in first degree relatives of affected individuals. In such cases awareness of the risk of the disease may prompt testing to achieve early diagnosis. Specific testing for genetic disease is an area of rapidly advancing knowledge (See Chapters 7, 8, 9, 10). In some cases genetic counselling and testing may have been offered to birth parents before adoption. Counselling is an important process that should be a precursor to testing in cases where information about possible genetic disease arises. The question of testing raises complex issues which are discussed in Chapter 13.

The development of technology brings some questions into sharp focus. *What are the rights of this child to be tested or not? How should one weigh up those rights against the rights of the birth family, or of the family that is going to take care of the child?*

Parents and professionals have no moral right to ask for a child to be tested unless a treatment or intervention is available for a suspected condition, for example, diabetes, where it is clearly in the child's best interests to be tested (see Chapter 14). Part of prospective adoptive parents' assessment and preparation for adoption and long-term care should be discussion of the issue of genetic disease and attitudes to the possibility of a child developing an inherited disorder. The financial and personal consequences for child and family of living with the threat of the onset of genetic disease as well as the implications of chronic illness, mental disease or retardation, and possibly the terminal illness of the child, must be considered. In many cases it may be necessary for all concerned to learn to live with uncertainty until the child is grown up. The child, when old enough to understand the implications of testing (after explanation), can give consent to testing on his or her own behalf when, in the opinion of the doctor being consulted, he or she can fully comprehend the implications of the tests.

Handling genetic information

Where there is a genetic concern about a child, professionals must consider the question:

How do you tell adoptive parents?

Which leads to subsidiary questions:

Who should tell?

What? When? And how do you convey uncertainty?

The medical adviser to the Adoption Panel should ensure that genetic issues are adequately discussed with specialist referral where necessary. It is important that the prospective adopters' social worker is also involved in this discussion. The degree of information given depends on the condition and how much is known. It is important not to overwhelm or alarm prospective adoptive parents but honest information should be offered and questions answered. This should happen as early as possible in the process of matching of child and family, *prior* to introduction and placement. Once the child and family have made contact it may be more difficult for new parents to weigh the significance of future difficulties against the current appeal of the child. Many people would rather feel that professionals had all the answers but in these circumstances it is vital for the medical adviser to be quite open about the level of uncertainty. The importance of uncertainty in adoption should be stressed by the social worker assessing the couple prior to approval. Uncertainty can be further discussed by the social worker on placing the child and reinforced by written medical information. Follow up appointments should be offered as required. Referral for further specialist advice should be considered wherever appropriate. These issues are covered in Chapters 2 and 3.

The careful compilation of genetic facts occurring around adoption has no parallel in the lives of healthy children who remain with the birth parents. One might ask:

How much difference could it make to the child if adoptive parents have more genetic information about them than birth parents would have?

Adoptive parents may receive health information that was not available to birth parents. At times this can be overwhelming and requires time to be digested. Few birth parents experience the task of getting to know so much about a child so quickly. Information is not always an advantage. A child with an increased risk of disorder may suffer from over-close surveillance. On the other hand, knowledge may allow for early intervention and prevention of some aspects of genetically determined disorder. Where there are problems with sensitive information it is possible for this to be stored for later access when necessary by the child or by an adult acting on their behalf. In future, stored genetic material from birth parents may be a direct source of information.

It is important that all professionals who work with children are wary of self-fulfilling prophecy and one should thus ask:
If adoptive parents are told about a possibility of genetically derived behaviour problems will this increase the likelihood of environmentally determined difficulty?
It is hoped that knowledge will reduce the risk of problems and for this reason information about constitutional factors that may be associated with behaviour difficulty cannot be withheld. The justification for giving information must be that a better understanding of a child's constitution allows for environmental factors to be optimised. It is important that new parents should be prepared for the eventuality that they may require professional help with behavioural problems. Where there is a constitutional difficulty, prior awareness by the adoptive parents should enable them to seek help without feeling that they have failed.

Special problems of confidentiality and disclosure have arisen as genetic science progresses and these raise complex questions like:
What should happen to genetic information that emerges after adoption?
Such information may have implications for the birth family for future pregnancies if an adopted child develops genetic disease. It could be important to inform the birth mother but this raises issues of confidentiality and of practicality (see Chapters 13 and 15). Similarly, a new diagnosis of genetic disease in the birth family has implications for the child but even if consent is obtained to pass this on, communication may be difficult in practice.

Working with genetic knowledge

Where a child has a hereditary disorder:

What help is available?

This book contains a directory of resources (see Appendices) and referral to a specialist genetic centre should be available at an early stage. Specialist advice on the implications of the disorder may be necessary for placement decisions. Treatment in most cases is directed towards symptoms rather than their cause, for example, drug treatment of epilepsy, but in a few conditions specific treatments are vital (eg phenylketonuria). New specific approaches such as 'gene therapy' are at a very early stage; specialist advice should be sought for an update on future options.

Developing genetic knowledge presents a challenge to the social sciences' emphasis on culture and environment. Experience in practice can lead to a shift of understanding. Medical geneticists and adoption professionals approaching each others' expertise with respect may find that this complex interface is not as readily polarised as the old arguments of nature versus nurture might suggest.

References

1 Littlewood R, 'Racism: Diagnosis and Treatment', *British Journal of Psychiatry*, 157:451-452, 1990.

2 McWhinnie A, and Batty D, *Children of Incest: Whose Secret Is It?*, BAAF, 1993.

2 A social work perspective

Marjorie Morrisson

The social worker plays a significant role in helping those involved in the adoption process to move through the different developmental phases they will experience. What are the specific concerns that social workers must consider when questions of genetic disease arise? This chapter explores these, and also discusses the implications for adoptive parents, and offers guidance on dealing with genetic conditions pre and post-placement.

The majority of social workers involved in the adoption process – whether around the time of placement for adoption or much later when counselling is sought about tracing and post-adoption questions – only occasionally find themselves confronted with issues of significant genetic concern. However, while the clinical geneticist may, in providing genetic counselling and using family trees, sometimes become conscious of the cross-over to adoption through identifying a family member separated through placement in a non-related family, the social worker in adoption is always aware that at the heart of adoption there is genealogical discontinuity. While the child's genetic inheritance is only one part of this, every adoptive family needs to work out the importance for themselves of the absent biological parents. In order to explain the different aspects of parenting to children, Vera Fahlberg,[1] an eminent US psychotherapist, uses three circles:

Life Sex determination Physical appearance Predisposition for certain diseases Intellectual potential Temperament Talents	Financial responsibility Safety & security Major decisions (to live, school, etc.) Consent for operations Other legal consents Legal responsibility for children's actions	Love, Discipline Daily needs (food, toys, clothes, etc.) Help with school work Take care of when sick Provide transport Life skills Values
Birth parent	*Legal parent*	*Parenting parent*

For adopted children, the roles of legal and parenting parent may be combined but they and their adoptive parents at different times may need to address the psychological impact of the separate genetic background.

There is an increasing wealth of material about adoptive parenting and the experiences of adopted people, including the recent publication *The Adoption Life Cycle* by Elinor Rosenberg.[2] What this highlights are stages in the life of the adoptive family and the particular factors within such families that distinguish them from other, non-adoptive, families including the developmental phases for birth parents, adoptive parents and adopted children, and the emotional issues linked to them. The social work task is about helping the different members of the adoption triad move through these developmental phases. Genetic issues, if they arise, may be significantly affected by progress in these areas. The purpose of the first part of this chapter is to explore briefly, with particular reference to the child's separate biological history within the adoptive family, the social worker's role in a number of areas:

– counselling relinquishing birth parents;
– assessing and preparing families for adoptive parenthood;
– identifying and supporting adoptive placements for children unable to remain with their biological parents;
– and offering post-adoption services.

Within this context the second part of the chapter will look at some of the concerns for social workers when questions of genetic disease occur.

As an introduction it is perhaps wise to remind ourselves of the very personal and often intense feelings of the individuals most intimately concerned. First, here is an extract from a poem written by an adoptive father 21 years ago followed by a comment recently made when looking back on it.

From Mark David
  Fleshed there in a strange womb
  Part of you, but not of us
  We waited as anxious guests
  On the threshold
  To come into your life . . .

'From the outset I was conscious of the fact that we had charge of his young life and that his birth parents were an integral part of Mark. Indeed as he grew older and his personality evolved I became increasingly conscious that there were genetic forces at work but that we had no point of reference with which to gauge this – a case for more open adoption in my opinion.'[3]

From a different perspective – that of the adopted person – the Scottish poet and playwright Jackie Kay wrote the following verse:[4]

I don't know what diseases
come down my line;
when dentist and doctors ask
the old blood questions about family runnings
I tell them: I have no nose or mouth or eyes
to match, no spitting image or dead cert,
my face watches itself in the glass

From secrecy to openness

The peak in numbers of children placed for adoption in Scotland was in 1972. The vast majority of children placed in non-related families were babies; it was largely a closed process with emphasis on confidentiality. Once the legal process of adoption was complete, it was felt that the adoptive family were entitled to the same privacy as any other family and any official outside involvement ended. In Scotland it was always possible for adopted people from the age of 17 to have access to their original birth certificates. In *In search of Origins*[5] published in 1973 and based on research in Scotland, Professor Triseliotis began the exploration of what lies behind the adopted person's search for knowledge of their birth parents. Since then, and with the legal changes that enabled adopted people in England and Wales to trace their origins, there has been a tremendous growth of interest in this area. From the experiences of these people has come a much deeper understanding that informs current practice.

Where a pregnant mother is considering adoption, the social worker has a dual task – to counsel the mother in making her decision and to gather information for the adoption panel and prospective family so that an appropriate decision is made. The research that is available about birth mothers who have relinquished children in the past shows the majority made the decision reluctantly due to circumstances outside their control. The social work task of accomplishing the twin areas of helping the birth parent and gathering the important information for the child may, in practice, therefore not prove quite so easy. There are helpful guidelines in *Children in Care: The medical contribution*[6] about gathering information. It is clearly *not* the role of the social worker to become a medical expert; rather, it is to use the agency medical adviser appropriately for guidance and continue to find a balance between sensitive response to very painful feelings of the birth parents and helping them understand the need to provide information.

Given the nature of the information sought it is not surprising that it often touches very emotive areas of family functioning. While studies have been done around the stages of grieving by relinquishing mothers, there is ample evidence from research that feelings may remain unresolved many years after placing a child for adoption.[7,8,9,10] Various studies have shown that the effects of relinquishment are experienced as negative and long-lasting. While the legal right of access to information that could assist in tracing lies only with adopted people, there is now increasing willingness to listen to the wishes of birth parents in this respect. A growing number of workers in post-adoption projects are prepared to go beyond a passive recording of the interest of birth parents to a more pro-active approach to adoptive parents or adopted people. There is now a much wider range of options for linking across the divide between the biological and adoptive families.

Publicity about openness in adoption has created anxieties in many people's minds lest some of the value of the *security* of adoption is lost by a less secretive approach. However, while regular contact is not normally the plan, there is greater attention paid to providing ways of adding to adoption records and building in exchange of information through post box mechanisms. In the long-term these changes may ease both the psychological resolution for birth parents and children separated by adoption and the need in some instances for sharing of medical or genetic information, but at present social workers are handling situations where there has been a gulf of many years. There also may be a need expressed by some individuals for further counselling at intervals, as the legitimacy of their original decision needs to be re-examined at critical life events.

The implications for adoptive parents

All this has tremendous implications for adoptive parents. *The Adoption Life Cycle*[11] is helpful in highlighting the developmental stages in building the adoptive family. This includes the move from the investigation of fertility problems, or in a few instances genetic counselling, to consideration of adoption acknowledging all the hopes and expectations that may have existed and the need to mourn the loss of bloodline and loss of their fantasised biological child. Author Elinor Rosenberg's view is that, 'If they continue to long for a biological child and have not accepted the validity of psychological parenting they will not be prepared to go the extra mile that proves their wholehearted permanent commitment to this child.'

Apart from the key area of embracing the differences in *adoptive* parenthood and the need to recognise the position of the biological parents, the range and nature of the children placed for adoption also need to be acknowledged. Inherent in this is the need to be able to accept risk, and be able to change and adjust if life does not go according to plan! Agencies vary in both the method and pace of conveying the potential challenges in adoption and the lack of guarantees to applicants. Some agencies are beginning to find that the number of applicants for babies and young children is falling, perhaps affected by the wider range of medical options, and those that choose adoption start from a more sophisticated understanding of the implications. Others hope that by sending out very explicit information about the needs of children being placed an element of self-selection will operate. For many years now agencies have been using various forms of groups alongside the traditional home study. Now there is increasing interest in systemic approaches to illuminate areas like family problem-solving mechanisms, family value systems, and communication networks, incorporating tools like genograms and eco-maps to help families explore these issues for themselves.[12] The hope of adoption workers is that by learning and building on such techniques we can make better judgements about appropriate placements for individual children and support the families more effectively.

Of course central to the work with families is ensuring that they are equipped to handle those issues peculiar to adoptive parenting, a crucial one being helping the child integrate their biological and adoptive history in a way that builds a healthy identity and self-esteem. The work done by Brodzinsky[13] in exploring children's understanding of adoption at different stages of development offers much clearer guidelines about this process. This progresses from the simple wish by the young child that they had come from their adoptive mother's tummy, through the growing awareness of the 8–12-year-olds of the feelings of others beyond themselves which can prompt a concern for birth parents, to the complex struggles of the adolescent to determine what kind of adult they can or will become. Sorting out what they have incorporated from the parenting offered by the adopters and what might be their genetic inheritance from biological parents can cause upsurges of interest in birth parents that can seem threatening to the adopters.

The time where the needs of these separate participants in the adoption triad are considered together is at the point of linking a child with a family. Where children have clearly identified needs – age, life-experiences, ethnic origin, disabilities – the criteria may be quite specific but what about comparatively straightforward babies where there is a wide choice of families? How much attention should be paid to aspects like physical characteristics of parents, intellectual potential and other basic personality traits or abilities that might have a genetic element?

There was concern a number of years ago that an emphasis on matching babies could collude with a wish of adoptive parents to claim the child as their own and pretend the biological parent did not exist. Some agencies moved to the position that any family well-prepared and assessed for the task should be able to undertake the adoption of a relatively straightforward baby and therefore, after considering any specific requests of the birth parents, it was fairer to simply start at the top of the waiting list of families. However, other agencies *are* taking into consideration matching factors having regard to likely genetic characteristics. While recognising that these only give broad parameters we know that there are some children who struggle with feeling very different from their family – either in appearance or abilities – and some adoptive parents find it hard to understand a child who is very different from themselves or anyone in their extended family. This is a complex area of hopes, expectations and living with reality. Some adoptive parents have said well after placement that a lot of time was spent with them discussing ways of helping children grow and change and redress possible earlier damaging experiences, but they also needed support in adjusting to living with what was inherent in the child. We still have a lot to learn about what happens when adopted people meet birth parents and what factors affect this. However, for some adopted people, looking for similarities – points of identification – plays a part. Those social workers who now acknowledge matching are, however, very clear that it can only be done following very careful preparation of the family about the *difference* in adoptive parenting and a very open acknowledgement of the biological parents.

Dealing with genetic conditions pre-placement

Given this broad context of current adoption practice, how do we deal with situations where significant genetic conditions are also involved? The issues will differ depending on whether a genetic condition has been identified prior to placement or emerges after the adoption has been finalised. In planning a placement for a child the genetic disorder may be known about from the outset and be part of the mother's considerations about placement or, it may be that the condition becomes apparent through the pre-adoption medical or the medical history gathered from the birth parents.

At this stage the social worker needs help from the agency medical adviser to understand not only the likely risk or prognosis for the child but also the implications for the birth parents; whether any further genetic counselling, and possibly testing, would be helpful and what the implications of this might be; what medical specialists would be available to talk to birth parents or adoptive parents, and what further medical supports might be needed or available.

Armed with this sort of information the social worker's initial task is to consider the birth parents. The social worker and the birth parent may be unprepared for a problem arising if it was not obvious at birth. If it is discovered that the mother has a genetic defect, what are the possibilities of her developing health problems in the future? Is this something that could have a bearing on future choices about reproduction? It takes little imagination to think of the effect of handling these questions in the midst of struggling with relinquishing a child for adoption.

A further complication arises if a condition identified in a child is known to be caused by a recessive gene carried by both parents. The birth mother may be resistant to revealing details about the birth father. How far and how hard does the social worker pursue this? What are the rights of the birth father for information that might be relevant for him? What extra information might be available that could add to the medical assessment for the child? The social worker's task then is to help unravel this juxtaposition of concerns and discover if in consequence the plan for the child needs to be reconsidered.

The next step is to explore the prospects for placement of the child. What do we know about placing children with medical conditions or disabilities? There is the encouragement of knowing that families have been found for a very wide range of children, many of whom have profound disabilities. However, it can take longer to identify the right placement. We know that the families who want to care for such children may not fit the traditional image of adopters. They may be single people, families who have already brought up children, or those with direct experience of disability. For the birth parent this can mean adjusting both their time scale and the image they have carried of this ideal family that offered the best future for their child.

Of course it is vital to know as much as possible about the prognosis for the child so that any placement identified has greatest chance of meeting the child's needs and the support network can be properly planned. Genetic conditions challenge us with a whole range of different possibilities. If a child is born with immediately recognisable disabilities we have a clear starting point. There is now a considerable amount of evidence about finding families for children with disabilities and research such as that described in *Against the Odds*,[14] by MacAskill, has shown some of the factors that recur. However, while we know that there can be considerable variation in the severity of conditions like Down's syndrome or spina bifida, people generally feel they have got some identifiable starting points in understanding the needs of children affected by such problems. The cause of them is secondary. Families applying to adopt often indicate an interest in a particular disability that is familiar to them but it may not be appreciated that some conditions have great variability in severity and outcome.

One group of children that presents itself fairly often as needing placement are those who are beyond babyhood and show clearly recorded developmental delay. Their history may include a combination of factors such as parents who required special schooling, high risk lifestyles and severe under-stimulation while in the care of birth parents, all of which may have implications for developmental outcome. In some cases screening for a condition like Fragile X syndrome may be suggested but at the end of the day a family is needed who can accept a child with no guarantees about their achievement potential.

Other children may appear normal at first but may be known to have the gene such as that causing Duchenne muscular dystrophy. They need a family who can plan ahead for the practical management of physical deterioration to life in a wheel-chair, and a shortened life expectancy, and also have the strength to handle the emotional demands which may arise. If the outcome is unclear at the placement, then some families who are geared to caring for a dependent child may not be appropriate or wish to be considered because of feeling that another family would be better if, in fact, the child progressed well and was able to lead a full active normal life.

Words like "late onset" and "life threatening" are significant ones that occur with some genetic conditions. Sometimes families – perhaps slightly older people – may come forward who respond particularly to the challenge of giving a child a happy loving experience of life knowing that the child is not expected to survive beyond childhood. These are people who are not approaching adoption from a *generational* viewpoint. They may already have children or even grandchildren. For other people who apply to adopt, the possibility of a late onset condition which may be life-threatening in adulthood would be very hard to contemplate. Their view of parenting may be strongly rooted in building up a family and thinking ahead to future generations. Some adoptive parents, because of their own vulnerable areas, may find it painful to consider having to support their adopted young people through decisions around reproduction if they carry a genetic defect.

The *risk* of developing an illness in the future presents other challenges. The condition that comes to mind here is schizophrenia where it may be the birth parents' psychiatric condition that has led to the proposed placement. People, of course, vary in the degree of risk they can accept. For example, reports on adoptive families may say that they can accept a child with one schizophrenic parent but not two. The social worker's task, however, is to explore beyond their level of tolerance of risk and look at questions like how they would approach mental health problems, the thought they have given to a supportive environment for the child, the sort of provisions they might make in case the adopted young person developed problems. A family might decide not to share very confidential information about the child with extended family members but would need to consider *their* attitudes to mental health so that the likelihood of support being available if needed is addressed.

Families prepared for an open approach to adoption will also need to explore whether the medical and genetic issues may affect their approach to meeting birth parents, giving information to the child about their adoption at different stages, particularly knowledge both of the reasons why the child was placed for adoption and the birth parents' life history, and guiding the young person who might want to consider tracing. Sometimes families who knowingly seek to take on the care of a child with a diagnosed genetic condition or risk offer to do this on a fostering rather than an adoptive basis suggesting that while they would be committed to the child's care they would feel more secure about the availability of support if the local authority retained some responsibility. The work done during the assessment and preparation period and the use of various methods to elucidate family communication systems, values, problem-solving strategies, adaptation to change and support networks, are the key to decision making.

Dealing with genetic issues post-placement

Another area where social workers may be involved is when genetic issues emerge well after placement. Sometimes the medical issue may be the spur to trying to bridge the divide between biological parent and the adopted child, for example, an adoptive parent seeking a blood relative who may be a suitable donor for an adopted child needing a bone marrow transplant; an adopted person trying to fill in gaps in medical history highlighted when undergoing medical investigation; a birth parent recently made aware of a family predisposition to a medical condition wanting to find out about the well-being of her child. At present in the majority of such situations there has been no ongoing link between birth parents and adoptive family. This is where an awareness of the stages that birth parents, adoptive families and adopted people move through is important because we usually do not know how far they have come in that process, or how well they have managed the different stages and therefore how they might respond.

As an illustration of this it might be helpful to go through the stages where a serious condition like Huntington's disease has been confirmed in a birth parent who has returned to the agency through which she had placed her daughter for adoption some years before. The social worker at this stage is likely to feel a high sense of anxiety and pressure to act on behalf of the adopted child and adoptive family. While the worker is struggling with this, the birth parent may well be in the throes of dealing with the re-emergence of all the pain of the relinquishment a number of years ago, together with anxiety about disrupting the security of a placement that she may have been comforting herself by seeing as perfect for her child. It is likely that the mother may already have received some counselling for herself and any other children she is caring for in relation to their own health issues and there may well have been a considerable time-lag before the mother felt able to acknowledge the implications for the relinquised child. While the planning of the next step needs to be approached very carefully, the time-scale also needs to recognise the anxiety for the birth parent concerned about the well-being of the adopted child.

The social worker at this point may not know much about the condition or what medical support and counselling services are available, how quickly an appointment can be arranged with a geneticist, what self-help groups might be around. He or she therefore needs to feel equipped to respond to the family's need for some information about the next steps. Then there are the practicalities about checking if there is any current contact with the family and the tracing required to try and establish their current address. The general experience of counselling is that it is usually best to send a brief letter arranging a contact. In wording this, there needs to be a balance between indicating that it is important for the adoptive family to respond without giving too much significant and emotive information in a letter. For example, the letter might indicate that the birth mother had been in contact and had provided further information about herself that she thought should be shared with the adoptive parents for the benefit of their child. Again the experience of adoption agencies who have established contacts on behalf of birth parents is that they have met a wide range of responses from positive to threats of solicitors' letters! Some people may be angry or distressed and it is useful to build in a way back for families who are initially too shocked to respond. Other families may request, and be able to use, both social work and medical services very quickly. Many aspects of the medical concerns will be similar to those that challenge biological parents.

There are, however, other factors that are special to the adoptive situation. They may be at a stage in their adoptive family life cycle when they feel challenged in their parenting and so it may be a difficult time to cope with added stresses which stem from the birth parents. The child or young person may be at a stage in handling their adoptive status when they are very aware of the lost birth parent or may be struggling with identity and what in general terms they have inherited from biological parents – as suggested in the Brodzinsky[15] stages. The adoptive parent may already be unsure about pacing the amount of detail about birth parents that is shared and with this new factor there is, of course, a vast new dimension. Associated with this is the sensitive area of the young person's future consideration of becoming a parent themself, given that the adopters may have painful memories of their own struggles in this respect.

There are, of course, no easy responses to these life-challenges. The Adoption Law Reviews in England and Wales and in Scotland acknowledge the need for post-adoption support services although there is need for much more detailed thought around allocation of resources stretching well beyond the current provisions for adoption allowances. Even a cursory consideration of the reality of adoptive parenthood indicates that we cannot be complacent about feeling the job is done when the adoption order is granted. Books like Ann Hartman's *Working with Adoptive Families beyond Placement*[16] encourage us to think about building on the techniques used during preparation to help families adjust at different stages and adapt to the reality of their placement. The families are only at the very beginning of a journey and they are entitled to expect that if the hurdles are there so, hopefully, will be the supports.

References

1 Fahlberg V, *A Child's Journey through Placement*, BAAF, 1994.

2 Rosenberg E, *The Adoption Life Cycle*, Free Press, 1992.

3 Scottish Adoption Advice Centre, Newsletter No.5 Poems – *Mark David*.

4 Kay J, *The Adoption Papers*, Bloodaxe, 1991.

5 Triseliotis J, *In Search of Origins*, Routledge & Kegal Paul, 1973.

6 Oxtoby M, (Ed) *Children in Care: The medical contribution*, BAAF, 1989.

7 Bouchier P, Lambert L, and Triseliotis J, *Parting with a Child for Adoption*, BAAF, 1991.

8 Howe D, Sawbridge P, and Hinings D, *Half a Million Women: Mothers who lose their children by adoption*, Penguin, 1992.

9 Winkler R, & Van Keppel M, *Relinquishing Mothers in Adoption*, Melbourne Institute of Family Studies, 1984, Australia.

10 Deykin E Y, Campbell L, and Patti P, 'The Post Adoption Experience of Surrendering Parents', *American Journal of Orthopsychiatry* 54, 1984, USA.

11 See 2 above.

12 Hartman A, *Finding Families: An ecological approach to family assessment in adoption*, Sage Publications, 1979.

13 Brodzinsky D M, Singer L M, and Braff A M, 'Children's Understanding of Adoption', *Child Development* 55, USA.

14 MacAskill C, *Against the Odds*, BAAF, 1985.

15 See 13 above.

16 Hartman A, *Working with Adoptive Families beyond Placement*, Child Welfare League of America, 1984, USA.

3   The role of the medical adviser

Dr Anne Grant

This chapter begins by tracing the development of medical input into the adoption process. Having considered recent changes, it then looks at the need for greater information about a child's genetic inheritance and addresses the question of why genetics should enter the adoption process. The implications on the health of a child with a known genetic history are discussed in some detail clearly pointing to the benefits that this information can provide. The gathering of this information is then explored with some recommendations on the role of the medical adviser in acting on the information supplied.

Medical input into the adoption process has been developing dramatically over the past decade since the implementation of the Adoption Agencies Regulations 1983 (England and Wales)[1] and Adoption Agencies (Scotland) Regulations 1984.[2] These regulations gave statutory recognition to the increasing complexity of the situations of the children currently being placed for adoption, with acknowledgement of the need for the appointment of such numbers of medical practitioners as were considered necessary for the purpose of providing the adoption agency with advice in connection with the exercise of its functions. This development followed the shift in the preceding decade away from the adoption within Britain of predominantly healthy, white babies towards the consideration of the feasibility of finding permanent homes for the many thousands of children who had previously been deemed 'unsuitable' for adoption – the older child, the child with medical or developmental problems, the black or mixed race child, the child with a family history of hereditary disease, and so on.

Prior to these comparatively recent developments, the medical input to the adoption process had concentrated largely on pronouncing babies as fit for adoption or not. As the supply of healthy, white babies began to diminish in the late 1960s to early 1970s, the concepts of 'special needs adoption' and the 'hard to place child' were born.[3] Rowe and Lambert, in the *Children who Wait* report of 1973 looked at 2,812 children in institutions in Britain, and postulated that there were around 7,000 children nationwide needing to be placed with a family; of these children, they found that 46 per cent had problems of health, physical defects, developmental/learning problems, behaviour problems, or genetic risk.[4]

Since the early 1980s, the direction in social work has been towards permanency planning for children at a fairly early stage if it is clear that a child will not be able to be brought up in his or her family of origin. Thus the institutions have emptied, and these children are now the children who are the subjects of the adoption and permanent care process today.

This change was the underlying reason for the introduction of more direct access by the adoption agencies to medical advice. This took the form of the appointment of a medical adviser who would obtain and interpret medical information, be an integral member of the adoption panel, be available to discuss the implications of any medical facts and provide appropriate information to adopters, professionals dealing with the child, and to the child where appropriate.

It has, however, become apparent over the years that much more is required for all adopted children than merely interpretation of their known medical or developmental problems. With the trend for more openness in adoption,[5] greater information about a child's genetic inheritance has not necessarily followed, and this may contain vital information which, if not gathered at the time of placement, may have significant and damaging repercussions in later life. There is also the consideration that it is the right of the adopted child to have as much information about the health history of his or her birth family as the non-adopted child, as far as is possible, so that he or she can have as much confidence in the provision of a family history on the many occasions throughout life when it is asked for, for example, at antenatal clinics, child surveillance clinics, etc.

Why should genetics enter the adoption process?

The gathering of information about a child's genetic endowment at the time of placement can have far reaching implications for the child's health and wellbeing both present and future, for the adoptive family, for the child's future offspring and for the wider birth family of the child. Carers may be considering adoption because of a risk of a serious genetically determined condition in any birth children of their own, and an understanding of this and any implications for the adopters' health should be taken into account (for example, late onset conditions such as Huntington's disease).

Let us consider the child's health first, both present and future. It must be borne in mind that many of these children have been in and out of the care system many times, and their own medical records may be sub-optimal; therefore, clues towards a condition which a child currently has, but of which he or she has no present symptoms, may come out of the family history taken at the time of placement. A family history may reveal a condition with variability of expression; that is, one which may be inherited from generation to generation with differing severity – examples of this being sensorineural deafness and neurocutaneous disorders (Tuberous Sclerosis, Neurofibromatosis, etc). In other words, the child in question may actually have a condition which causes them no problem at present, but which may cause problems in the future, and which, in both of these cases, could have serious implications for future generations; the condition might be passed on in a much more serious form. An awareness of the family history can ensure that investigations are carried out to ascertain as far as possible whether in fact the child is affected. Diagnoses may also become 'lost' with the moves in and out of the care system (the parent held child health record will hopefully do much to alleviate this); a carefully taken family history may bring to light conditions which it is essential that any carer should know about for the future health of the child. For example, it is obviously essential that a diagnosis of a mild bleeding disorder should follow a child, but even this has been known to disappear in the mists of extreme social disorder.

When considering the future health, both mental and physical of the child, it is important that the adoptive parents should be aware of any late onset conditions either known to affect the child, or for which the child has an increased risk of inheritance. An obvious example of this is where either one or both birth parents suffer from schizophrenia. The future wellbeing of a young adopted adult developing schizophrenia may be much helped by the fact that he or she has been placed with parents who, at the time of placement, had a willingness to support that child should the tendency to mental illness be realised. For other late onset conditions, early diagnosis with treatment, therapies and counselling may be helpful, and may not be offered in the absence of an appropriate history. There is also the more straightforward factor of making the adopters aware, as parents, of a certain condition with a familial mode of inheritance being present in the birth family.

It is impossible to leave the area of future health without also considering the implications for those involved in the adoption process alongside the huge advances being made in the study of genetics over the past few years, and the development of more and more screening tests for certain population groups at risk. With the non-adopted population, most people have access to information on family medical history which enables them to find out if a condition with hereditary implications is, or was, present; the adopted person to date has rarely been able to do this. By the time that this generation of adopted children are in their middle age, who is to say whether or not prophylactic treatment may be available for certain at risk groups, for example, those with a family history of certain conditions for which such treatment does not currently exist; if the adopted person does not know of the existence of this condition in their family, they will be denied the opportunity to extend their life expectancy.

Advances in the identification of at risk groups in the population will of course also have implications for potential adoptive parents undergoing the process of registration as adopters; with advances in the knowledge of genetics, and with the advent of more accurate prediction of problems, there is a likelihood that medical advisers will be in the situation more frequently of being asked at panels about genetic risks to adults, and of seeking advice from geneticists about health aspects of potential adopters. However, this course of action has to be finely balanced between having the best interests of the child at heart, and being intrusive and distressing to the adult concerned. The whole area is fraught with sensitive issues; if a couple seeking to adopt have firstly undergone the traumas, perhaps, of coming to terms with infertility, must they now be faced with detailed enquiry and possible investigation in relation to genetic risk? They may well have been aware of risk factors in their family (to a degree), but might in normal circumstances have opted not to ascertain the exact risks, especially if no preventive health measures can be taken.

Risks to the future offspring of an adopted person can often be estimated at the time of placement, and failure to do this may cause much misery in later life. With improved carrier detection techniques and prenatal testing for serious disorders, it is imperative that the adopted person be given as much and as accurate information about his or her family as possible. The girl who has a brother with Fragile X syndrome, and is a carrier for the condition but unaware of this because the correct diagnosis has not been ascertained, will be devastated on giving birth to an affected child to know that prenatal diagnosis would have been available had she been aware of her family history. An adopted person with a family history, say, of Tuberous Sclerosis, even if little affected himself or herself, should have this information so that they can seek genetic counselling prior to starting a family. Children with parents belonging to the ethnic groups at risk of passing on the haemoglobinopathy gene(s) must be made aware of their situation, and counselling offered where appropriate.

There may be situations where a child may have on record the existence of the most severe and alarming conditions in, say, a sibling; the exact diagnosis and mode of inheritance of this condition may reassure that there is no risk whatsoever to future generations. This may occur in autosomal recessive conditions where the risk of recurrence only relates to future offspring of the birth parents. It is important to clarify this at an early stage, or it may cause great concern prior to and throughout pregnancy.

Naturally, potential adoptive parents want to have as full a history of the child's family medical background as possible; increasingly nowadays adopters are coming forward who are willing to adopt children with significant disabilities, for example Down's syndrome, or children with the risk of serious conditions; but it is a right, and indeed a legal expectation, that potential adopters should be given as much information about the background family and health history as possible, so that they have the opportunity to discuss whether they feel able to cope with this particular problem. Children with a risk of inheriting schizophrenia, for example, should only be placed with adoptive parents who have been given the opportunity to gain extensive knowledge about this condition, and who feel able to cope with this in their child should the need arise. There may justifiably be profound resentment if any information relating to the child's history, which could have been made available at the time of placement, was not.

Finally, the investigation of the family genetic history at the time of placement may identify areas where advice may be offered to members of the child's birth family, if a situation is uncovered which would be helped by genetic counselling. Time spent at this stage may save a very lengthy, difficult and often impossible task many years later if a significant genetically inherited condition comes to light either in the adopted person, or in a member of the family of origin.

Gathering the information

In the situation of the adoption process, this is beset with problems. The ideal, in clinical genetics, would be to construct a full and detailed family tree. This would generally start with the proband or affected individual, or the consultand, the person seeking advice – this person would be seeking advice because he or she knew of the existence in the family of a condition with a diagnosis attached to it, which was causing concern. Full details of the family and extended family would then be gathered, with members being invited for interview and examination where relevant, with investigations being carried out where appropriate. Information would be gathered about stillbirths, infant deaths and miscarriages; the causes of death within the family would be noted and checked where possible.

In the adoption situation, we start with a child who may or may not be perfectly healthy, with a family about whom there may or may not be any prior indication of reasons for concern. The medical adviser, therefore, is in the situation of trying to decide, from the available information, if there is anything in the family history about which further investigation is needed or about which further advice should be sought.

Crucial to this decision, therefore, will be the adequacy of information available. Frequently in the adoption process there are huge gaps in the information – the ideal would include details (name, age, date of birth, ethnic origin, state of health, diagnosis of any illness and/or date and cause of death) of parents, siblings, half siblings, parents' siblings and their children and grandparents. The situation is much complicated by the fact that many of the birth families of adopted people have multiple relationships thus producing very complicated family trees; obviously when assessing risk it is vital to know the exact relationship of one member of the family to another; also, in the case of contested adoption there may be refusal by the parent to divulge any information about their family. However, in many situations there may well be another relative, for example, a grandparent, who has been maintaining access to the child, and who may be willing to provide details about family history when the importance of this to the future of the child is explained.

It can be argued that medical advisers to adoption panels should strive towards the ideal; when one considers the enormous volume of information which generally accompanies each child to an adoption panel, spanning the whole of the child's life, it must surely be possible for more information on the family medical history to be gathered along the way. This is more likely to happen if social work colleagues have a knowledge and understanding of the importance of this aspect of the work, and in this area the medical adviser can be central to the development of good practice.

Acting on the information

Being in receipt of the child's family history, the medical adviser has then to decide whether there is any condition about which advice needs to be given concerning the likelihood of the child developing the condition; whether advice can be given about risks of a condition occurring in future generations; whether to seek further advice from the regional genetic centre; and whether as a result of the information gathered the child should undergo further investigations for a certain condition, or further information should be sought about a specific member or members of the family. The importance at this stage of easy access to a regional genetics centre for further advice, and for discussion of problems cannot be emphasised too strongly.

As far as is possible, the medical adviser will wish to check diagnoses, perhaps liaising with hospital or general practice colleagues, or asking the social worker for the child to ascertain certain extra facts. In the absence of a definitive diagnosis in a particular case, aspects of an individual's situation may make it possible to exclude certain diagnoses – they may be too well for a certain condition, too young for another, or too old still to be alive with another.

Table 1 lists a few of the common conditions encountered in family histories, and seeks to demonstrate the plethora of conditions with significant potential sequelae to the child and his or her family, both present and future, which may be suggested by a fairly simple statement about the health of a relative. The list could be extended to include the conditions arising in every system of the body; the lesson to be learned is that the medical adviser has to be alert to all possible diagnoses in the child's family history, and to be seeking optimal information to help towards an accurate assessment of the situation. Also, it underlines the importance for the medical adviser of having a comprehensive family history from the Social Worker undertaking the task of gathering the information.

These three examples have been selected as being fairly typical of the type of non-specific statement about the health of a relative which may emerge from the documentation concerning the background of a child at the time of adoption. Obviously, where the history is of a specific diagnosis such as diabetes, spina bifida, cleft palate, etc, in a relative or relatives, this poses less in the way of investigative problems, but still requires to be further explored in terms of the extent of the condition in the family, and advice needs to be sought regarding implications for the child.

When the picture has been drawn up as completely as possible, the facts will then be presented and explained to the other members of the panel when the child is considered for registration for adoption. Any needs the child has, both present and anticipated, can then be evaluated. The question of counselling for potential adopters must be considered at this stage, and a decision taken as to who would be the most appropriate person to do this. Frequently, when the situation is fairly straightforward, the medical adviser will choose to do this; however, it may be more appropriate to nominate either a specialist in a particular field, or a clinical geneticist.

Table 1

Family History of	Consider . . .	Further information required	Possible action
Learning Difficulties	– familial (part of normal distribution) – autosomal dominant – autosomal recessive – X linked conditions – chromosomal abnormalities – environmental factors eg. teratogens	– how many affected? – relationship to adopted child? – sex of those affected? – any known diagnosis? – child's development to date? – any other signs in affected relatives (part of a syndrome?)	– further discussion with family? – permission to investigate diagnosis of affected person(s)? – permission to contact GP/consultant of affected person(s)? – advice from clinical geneticist? – counselling for potential adopters? – counselling for natural family?
Deafness	– autosomal recessive – autosomal dominant – X linked condition – syndrome with deafness as a part of disorder? – prenatal infection? (eg. rubella) – late onset conditions	– conductive or sensorineural? If sensorineural loss:- – who is affected? – relationship(s) to adopted child? – age of onset? – sex of those affected? – any known diagnosis? – child's hearing normal? – any other signs/symptoms in affected relatives? (syndromes?)	– further discussion with family? – permission to investigate diagnosis of affected person(s)? – permission to contact GP/consultant of affected person(s)? – test child's hearing? – advice from clinical geneticist? – counselling for adoptive parents? – counselling for birth parents?
Blindness/vision problems	– autosomal recessive – autosomal dominant – X linked condition – syndromes with visual impairment? – late onset problems – prenatal problems	– who is affected? – relationship(s) to adopted child? – sex of those affected? – age of onset? – any known diagnosis? – other associated signs/symptoms? (syndrome?) – child's eyes/vision tested?	– further discussion with family? – permission to investigate diagnosis of affected person(s)? – permission to contact GP/consultant of affected person(s)? – arrange ophthalmological examination of child? – advice from clinical geneticist? – counselling for adoptive parents? – counselling for birth family?

It is vitally important that the material gathered is preserved and made available to the adoptive parents, thereby to be passed on to the child. This must include not only the history of conditions felt to be of clinical and genetic relevance to the child at present and to future offspring, but also, for the reasons discussed previously, the complete family history relating to the state of health and causes of death within the family. Obviously, this information must also be passed on to the child's future general practitioner.

Conclusion

Genetics in the adoption process is far from straightforward; in fact, it is a veritable minefield of complexity. Legal, ethical and confidentiality issues abound, and are addressed elsewhere in this book. Huge information gaps may exist, ranging from an incomplete family history to a total lack of information about one or both parents – the mother may be unwilling to divulge the identity of the father; she may be uncertain as to who he is; or the father's identity may be unknown in the case of a child born as the result of rape. The most extreme example of a complete lack of information would be the situation arising in the placement of the abandoned baby. Mothers may disappear during the placement process making the gathering of information difficult if not at times impossible. Other dimensions may come into the equation, such as the suspicion that the child may be born as a result of an incestuous relationship, with the resultant genetic implications. Frequently, questions are asked about the possible teratogenic effects (ie. causing abnormal development of the foetus) of excessive alcohol ingestion during pregnancy, or the self administration of drugs. Large, chaotic and disordered families are often encountered, with multiple partners in all generations and branches of the family.

However, it is becoming more and more widely accepted that it is expected that workers in the field of adoption, and medical advisers to adoption panels in particular, will strive towards the best practice in the provision of as complete a genetic history as possible for adopted people, with appropriate advice and counselling being given. It is of vital importance that this section of society, who have been denied the right, through circumstances outwith their control, to be brought up by their families of origin, should not then be further disadvantaged by being divorced from information about their genetic heritage.

References

1   BAAF Practice Note 5, *Medical aspects of the Adoption Agencies Regulations 1983* (England and Wales), BAAF.

2   BAAF Practice Note 9, *Medical aspects of the Adoption Agencies (Scotland) Regulations 1984 and the related court rules*, BAAF.

3   Wedge P, and Thoburn J, (eds), *Finding Families for 'Hard-to-place' Children*, BAAF, 1986.

4   Rowe J, and Lambert L, *Children who Wait*, BAAF, 1973.

5   Mullender A, *Open Adoption*, BAAF, 1991.

4 Practice examples of genetic disease within adoption

Dr Peter Turnpenny

Using several case examples, this chapter brings to the fore some of the difficulties that can arise as a result of genetic disease emerging in adopted people, birth parents, and sometimes others. Each case is followed by a comment on the pertinent issues arising from that case.

In this chapter an attempt is made to illustrate some of the difficulties that can arise as a result of genetic disease emerging in adopted people or birth parents, or indeed other involved individuals. The cases that follow are real cases with some adjustment of minor details to reduce the possibility of the families and individuals being identifiable. Although written from the medical geneticist's viewpoint, such cases are equally likely to be encountered within the practice of the medical adviser, adoption social worker, or family doctor. Indeed, some of the referrals came from social workers, medical advisers, or general practitioners. They are essentially a consecutive series of cases collected prospectively and can therefore be regarded as a reasonably representative sample of difficulties and dilemmas. The questions raised by these cases do not have easy or 'right' answers and, in general, responses are determined by a society's values and knowledge of the issues, which evolve over time. (In the pedigree diagrams square symbols represent males, circles females, and shaded symbols affected cases.)

Case 1
A GP called a clinical geneticist to say that his patient, an adopted person, was pregnant, and had been told that her biological grandfather suffered from 'muscular dystrophy'. An urgent appointment at the genetic clinic was arranged and the patient expressed great anger about the fact that she knew she was adopted but had never been told the family history. Using written permission from the patient, the Family Finding Centre was

approached and the name and birth date of the biological mother, and the name of the grandfather, were obtained. He was described as having 'muscular dystrophy' and confined to a wheelchair. The information was extremely scant and it was therefore desirable to verify the diagnosis and obtain more medical details.

The search began and over the next few weeks some 25 telephone calls were made to the following: the Registrar of Births, Marriages and Deaths Office; the Central Register of GPs; several hospital records departments; several Primary Care departments and general practitioners. Because of the sensitive and confidential nature of the enquiry, copies of various records were sent by recorded delivery and many people devoted a lot of time to the task. Finally the right records were unearthed and it emerged that the grandfather did not have 'muscular dystrophy' after all, and so the patient who had been adopted could be reassured after several anxious weeks of pregnancy when she was wondering what the implications were for herself and offspring.

Comment
The woman was justifiably concerned and anxious about the family history, especially now that she was pregnant. It would have been much more straightforward to investigate the family history without the pressure of her pregnancy, so ideally she should have been informed much earlier. The information given to her proved to be inaccurate but caused huge anxiety and resulted in many people giving a great deal of time to the case. The importance of communicating accurate information is highlighted by this case.

Case 2
A 30-year-old woman (Fig. 1, III.2) at 50 per cent risk for Huntington's disease attended the genetic clinic for counselling leading towards a predictive gene test. Her older sister (III.1) had died as a teenager, already showing clear signs of the disease, before their father (II.1) developed symptoms himself. This affected father (II.1) had been adopted but it was possible to gather information about the extensive biological family history which left no doubt about the diagnosis, and the adopted man's father (I.1) was the affected grandparent of III.2. The result of the

Figure 1

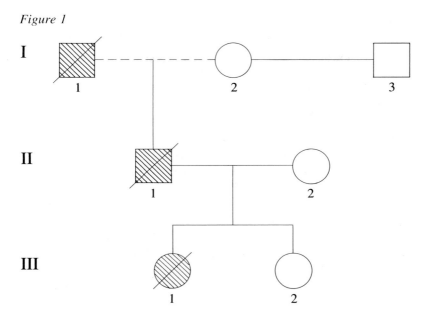

predictive test for the woman appeared to be negative because the 'large' DNA band characteristically associated with Huntington's disease was not present. However, only *one* normal band was present when two are expected. This can be explained by the two bands being of identical size, which appeared to be the case. However, in order to prove this beyond reasonable doubt it was decided to test the consultand's unaffected mother (II.2) from one side and her unaffected living grandmother (I.2) from her father's side – her father had died a number of years earlier and no DNA was stored from him. Testing her mother presented no problem but the consultand had no contact with her biological grandmother from her father's side, even though she lived nearby. The consultand knew that her grandmother was aware that her son, given up to be adopted, had died of Huntington's disease, but also knew that her grandmother's husband (I.3) had never been told about the adoption. The grandmother's GP was therefore approached confidentially to ask if he would request a blood sample from her, for the benefit of her biological descendents, when she next attended the surgery.

Comment

This case highlights the way in which new genetic techniques make it desirable sometimes to make contact with biological relatives. Here there was some risk of breaching confidentiality if great care had not been taken to approach the grandmother (I.2) in a way that created no suspicions for her husband (I.3).

Case 3

A 27-year-old mother (Fig.2, II.3) at 50 per cent risk for Huntington's disease attended the genetic clinic for counselling leading towards a predictive gene test. Her father (I.2) was institutionalised in the advanced stages of the condition, his earlier violence and difficult behaviour having been a major factor in the break up of his marriage to I.3. Prior to his marriage, and before he became symptomatic, he had a relationship with I.1 who gave birth to his child, II.1, and they moved away. No contact was kept with I.1 and her whereabouts, as well as those of II.1, are completely unknown to any family member. There is no opportunity, therefore, to present II.1 with information about Huntington's disease and

Figure 2

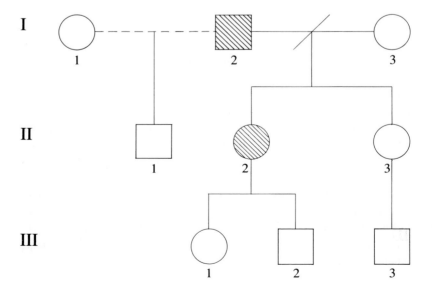

explain that he is at risk. If he has children of his own he is likely to do so in complete ignorance of the family history.

Comment

This is a potentially common scenario in the aftermath of an adoption placement, although in this case it does not relate strictly to a child (II.1) who lost contact with his affected parent for this reason. If he was traceable a new dilemma would present itself, namely whether it is the right and appropriate course of action to inform him about his father's illness.

Case 4

A 65-year-old woman (Fig.3, II.4) was finally given a clinical diagnosis of Huntington's disease after many years of exhibiting involuntary movements. This was subsequently confirmed by a direct gene test. The only family medical history known was from the death certificates of her parents, which indicated that her mother (I.2) died aged 60 from heart disease, and her father (I.1) aged 82 after a stroke. No mention was made

Figure 3

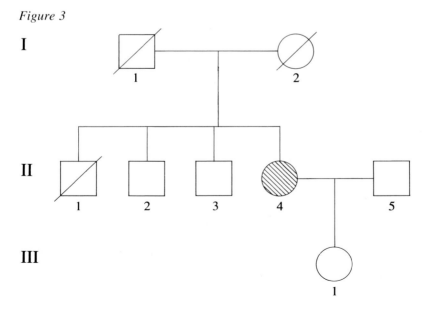

of a neurological disorder. As a young schoolchild, II.4 had been placed in foster care for reasons unknown to her and despite being raised in the same town as her parents, never saw them again. She also lost touch with her brothers (II.2,II.3) many years ago.

Comment
This case again highlights the lack of information resulting from the separation of family members. Here the reasons for the children (II.1 – II.4) being taken into foster care are unknown but one inevitably speculates on the possibility that Huntington's disease, in one guise or another in one of the parents, was responsible. It would be most helpful if the medical records of the parents had been kept, in order to scrutinise them for evidence of Huntington's, but current practice is to destroy death files after a period of time.

Case 5
An 11-year-old boy, who had been adopted as an infant was brought for reassessment on account of a malformation syndrome with the features of an underdeveloped right jaw, hearing deficit, a short right arm and absent right thumb. These defects were present from birth but the adoptive parents were keen for up-to-date information. The condition is usually sporadic, meaning that the risk of him having affected offspring in the future is low. However, some cases of parent to child transmission have been described. His birth mother certainly showed no evidence of the problem but she had refused to talk about the child's father at the time of the adoption. In the absence of further information the risk to the child's offspring in the future was given as 'low', with advice that he should return for further genetic counselling when he is an adult.

Comment
This case is typical of those where it is desirable to have complete information about a biological relative, in this instance the boy's father, in order to give the most accurate genetic risk assessment. It raises the question of whether the father's identity should be revealed by the mother, even though this is against her wishes.

Case 6

A 44-year-old woman (Fig. 4, I.2) brought her 10-year-old mentally disabled son (II.3) for assessment with a view to reaching a diagnosis, which had hitherto been elusive. Developmental delay had been apparent from infancy. Again, however, the cause of his disability was not apparent but there was certainly a possibility that it might be genetic and due to damage in an X-linked gene. If so, there would be a chance of his mother being a carrier. Realising this, her main concerns centred on her 'normal' daughter (II.2), who could also be a carrier with the risk of having a son with a mental disability one day. Fragile X syndrome was excluded. In discussing the family history she confided that she gave up a son for adoption (II.1) following a relationship before her marriage to I.1, about which her husband (I.3) was totally ignorant. If it was found that the adopted son had subsequently had developmental problems this would be potentially important genetic information for II.2. A confidential letter to the appropriate adoption social worker, using the mother's previous name, failed to identify any trace of the placement having been made, let alone any medical information about II.1.

Comment

There was no reason to doubt the story of I.2 and yet there was no trace of II.1's adoption. Whilst there may be a perfectly good explanation for

Figure 4

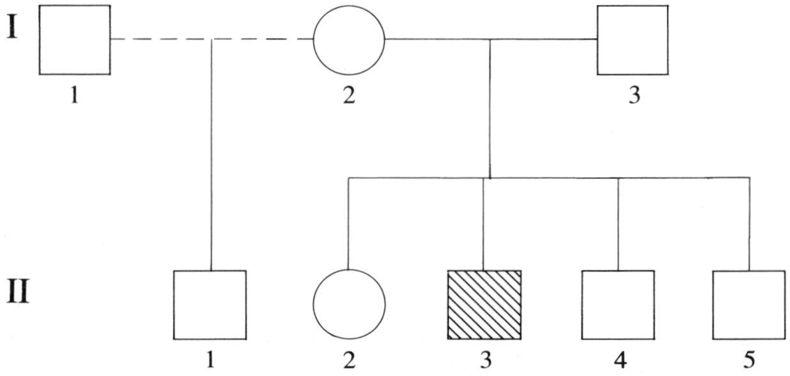

this it is possible that important records have been lost or misplaced. Safe and secure records are an essential part of good adoption practice.

Case 7

A woman gave birth to a child shortly after the diagnosis of neurofibromatosis (NF) had been made in her. She had additional features suggestive of another disorder occasionally associated with NF, which included a form of congenital heart disease. On questioning her about the family history it emerged that she had given birth to a child some 11 years earlier who had been adopted. NF is transmitted as an autosomal dominant, therefore the adopted child was at 50 per cent risk for this disorder and also, as it happens, for the variant which can cause congenital heart disease. Despite the adopted child's name having been changed it proved surprisingly easy to locate the medical notes without going through the local social work channels. In the adoption medical examination prior to placement there was no evidence for NF but this would not be expected at such an early age. However, the paediatrician commented on some slightly unusual facial features, which, with hindsight, might be a sign of the additional disorder. It was judged important to try and obtain some more details about the child and pass the information on to the adoptive parents at least. The GP was contacted but he deemed it unwise to make any approaches to the family.

Comment

Several issues are raised here:

1. The birth mother must have had clear signs of NF at the time of the adoption (such is the nature of NF) but no medical examination was carried out on her prior to the placement – indeed, there are no requirements to do so;
2. The examining paediatrician suspected unusual facial features but the significance was overlooked and no further opinion was sought. This should not be regarded as negligent because the 'range of normality' in the facial features of young infants is very wide. Conversely, it is also very difficult to diagnose many syndromes at this age because clearer features may not emerge until later childhood;

3. It was far too easy for medical staff to discover the adopted person's new identity from the medical records;
4. Should the GP have had the 'right' to block the flow of information to the adoptive parents?

Case 8

A 40-year-old woman, who had given a daughter up for adoption 13 years previously, was diagnosed as having a form of muscular dystrophy. The risk of her daughter inheriting this problem was 50 per cent, or 1 in 2. The birth mother expressed the wish that the information be conveyed to her daughter and the adoption social worker contacted the adoptive parents, who in turn discussed the matter with a clinical geneticist by telephone. The daughter apparently manifests no symptoms of muscular dystrophy but it is still possible that she might develop signs and symptoms at a later age. She was fully aware of her status as an adopted person but the adoptive mother felt that it would be more appropriate to pass the information on to her in four or five years' time.

Comment

There is no criticism of either the procedure or planned course of action here. The decision to communicate the genetic risk at age 17-18, rather than immediately, is based on the best judgement of the adoptive mother. It is not known, when the time comes, whether it will still be judged the best timing. A slowly increasing number of professionals are likely to know her genetic risk while she remains ignorant – will she resent this? Could the passage of time before disclosing the information result in tension within the adoptive family? Or is it because of existing subliminal tension that the adoptive mother wants to wait? In the event of her entering a sexual relationship with a boyfriend will this affect the timing and way in which the genetic risk is discussed?

Case 9

The adoption services are trying to place a child of 12 months who was born following an incestuous relationship between a brother and sister who were separated and fostered as children because of family and social problems. Both of them had learning difficulties and required special schooling. When they met up again in their late teenage years they were sexually attracted to each other. Their own parents were also of limited ability with low IQ. The child to be placed was born at full term after a normal pregnancy and there were no problems in the neonatal period. However, by late infancy there were some suspicious, though borderline, signs that he might not be performing quite as expected in terms of his developmental milestones, although his eyesight and hearing were normal. On examination there were no particular features to suggest a mental retardation syndrome and Fragile X was ruled out by appropriate tests. A second developmental assessment also raised questions about his performance but a third, some three months later by another paediatrician, suggested that his level was appropriate for age. The adoption services advised that it was not going to be feasible for the child's birth parents to be medically examined. Meanwhile adoptive parents were found for him and he was placed in the knowledge that ongoing monitoring of his performance would be indicated.

Comment

The problem of incest in the adoption circle is a very familiar one and the difficulties and dilemmas of this case are fairly typical. No reason for the educational subnormality in the family has been identified but a genetic cause is certainly possible, if not likely. When the early developmental assessment is borderline it is very difficult to predict final outcome. In this case, happily, adoptive parents were found but children like this are generally very difficult to place as most prospective adoptive parents want some basic reassurances that the child is healthy and likely to attend normal school.

Case 10

A baby was born with a cleft lip and palate after a normal pregnancy but in every other way appeared healthy and his subsequent development was normal. The couple already had one normal child, so the birth of their second with this relatively common but unsightly defect came as quite a shock. Both parents were healthy, neither having had a similar problem. However, the mother was herself adopted for reasons that she did not know, and she knew nothing about her birth parents. For most of her adult life she had a strong curiosity about her biological family and was well aware that she could seek their identity if she wished. The birth of her son with cleft lip and palate caused this curiosity to intensify – more than ever she wanted to discover her biological and social roots. However, she was also very hesitant about taking action, not knowing whether such a move would be in her, or her birth parents', best interests.

Comment

This woman's experience, in terms of her strong desire to know her origins, is a very familiar one both to adopted people and those who counsel individuals who are 'searching'. We should not be at all surprised if the desire to know one's origin is intensified at or around the time of preparing to become, or actually becoming, a parent oneself. The case highlights that 'genetic' as well as 'social' origins are immensely important to some adopted people and, indeed, often cannot be separated.

Case 11

A 28-year-old man (Fig.5, I.3) was investigated because of learning difficulties and found to have Fragile X syndrome, which is inherited as an X-linked condition with males manifesting features strongly and 'carrier' females sometimes showing mild features. His sister (I.2) therefore had a 50 per cent chance of being a carrier but was unavailable for counselling with a view to being tested. However, from the few details available there was a suspicion that she was a carrier. At least three children of hers (II.1–II.3) had been adopted as infants, and there was some information that II.1 had learning and behavioural difficulties. The two sisters, II.2 and II.3, were adopted together and their adoptive parents contacted. They attended for genetic counselling shortly afterwards, aged 17 and 18 years respectively. One decided later to be tested while the other preferred to wait until she was older. For both of them the original information that they might be at high risk of having retarded sons came as a shock.

Comment

The case illustrates that genetic disease in the wider family of a birth

Figure 5

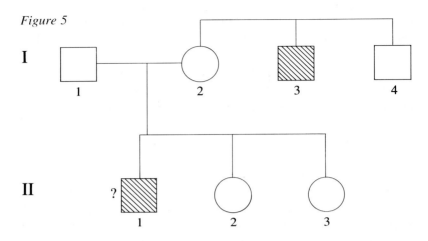

mother may have highly significant implications for the adopted children and, in turn, their children. Suddenly, the possibility of the girls being carriers of a gene for a disabling condition, for which they can opt to be tested, and also opt for prenatal testing in the future if they are carriers, confronts them. However, it would have been much more satisfactory if the diagnosis had been confirmed in their biological mother (I.2). The diagnosis was suspected clinically but if there had been no suggestive signs, and she was unwilling to be tested, the counselling for the adopted girls would have been more difficult. The importance of thorough and accurate genetic counselling cannot be emphasised enough for the condition of Fragile X. It is not enough just to organise a blood test without detailed explanation.

Case 12

A five-year-old girl was referred to the clinical genetics service for a specialist opinion in an attempt to reach a definitive diagnosis on her condition, which appeared to be a rare type of muscular dystrophy. The parents were first cousins, once removed, and themselves showed no evidence of the condition affecting their daughter. Their social circumstances had been significantly disrupted in the past and an earlier child, a son, had been adopted at the age of two years. They knew very little about him but there was a suggestion he might also have had the muscular dystrophy. In order to give accurate diagnosis and genetic counselling it was therefore considered important to trace this boy, now 13 years old. It was, in fact, possible to do this through the adoption agency and he was found to have the condition. However, care was required to preserve confidentiality because the boy was unaware that he had a full sibling elsewhere, something which the adoptive parents had not yet revealed. Reaching a definitive diagnosis was possible, thus allowing important information about genetic risk to be given to the birth parents at the time, and the affected individuals in the future.

Comment
This case is a good example of the importance of precise diagnosis in assessing genetic risk. In order to achieve this there was no alternative to tracing the adopted boy and conducting a clinical examination. However, there were some confidentiality risks attached to this which, fortunately, were surmountable.

Figure 6

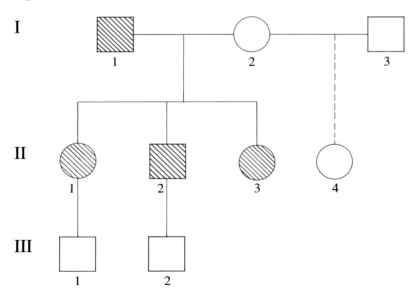

Case 13

A 48-year-old woman (Fig.6, I.2), divorced and remarried, had fostered a severely mentally disabled 10-year-old child (II.4) for many years. Her birth father lived overseas and had not seen her for several years. The woman (I.2) felt it was time to formalise the process and adopt the girl, for whom she was caring well. However, just as the application was being processed one of her three children (II.1–II.3) by her marriage to I.1 was diagnosed as having myotonic dystrophy, a form of muscular dystrophy with some wasting, weakness, and a variety of other problems. Very soon it was apparent that all the children, as well as their father (I.1), were affected. Indeed, her daughter (II.1) was quite moderately affected and expecting a baby (III.1). The condition is slowly progressive but with all the children showing clear signs of the disease in their early twenties there was the prospect that they would be quite weak and requiring all kinds of support within 10-20 years. This prospect raised the uncertainty about the wisdom of adopting II.4, as I.2 might increasingly be called upon to care for her birth children.

Comment

This case presents an example of how a genetic disease can affect the prospects for adoption indirectly. The physical and mental health of the adoptive parent(s) is extremely important but so too is the health of others for whom she may be responsible. She has been most unfortunate to have all three of her birth children affected by this condition which is inherited in an autosomal dominant manner.

Case 14

A woman in her mid-fifties was being regularly followed up in a medical clinic for familial hypercholesterolaemia, from which a number of her first degree relatives had died in their late forties. The condition results from an inherited enzyme defect and the outcome is a raised blood cholesterol which predisposes to premature atherosclerotic heart disease. Those affected are at high risk of early death from myocardial infarction in their forties or fifties (see Chapter 10). This woman's blood cholesterol was kept under control by new drug therapy. Twenty years earlier she and her husband were unable to have children and tried to adopt.

However, with the diagnosis and known family history, the adoption agency sought advice about her suitability as an adoptive mother. No effective therapy was available and she was judged unsuitable on the grounds that she was unlikely to be able to raise a child to the threshold of adulthood. Her desire to bring up a child therefore remained unfulfilled, a decision which deeply affected her ever since.

Comment
This case illustrates the point that the health of adoptive parents must be taken into consideration in a placement. This woman was healthy when she and her husband applied to be adoptive parents but was known to have a high cholesterol level with a family history which mitigated against her. It could not have been confidently foreseen that an effective drug therapy would emerge for her condition, so the judgement was made in good faith. One can also imagine the scenario of a prospective adoptive mother at 50 per cent risk of Huntington's disease who would have been denied the opportunity to adopt in the days before it was possible to perform genetic testing. Adoption panels, and especially medical advisers, have to make decisions based on present knowledge. However, advances are so rapid in medical science that some decisions, with hindsight, may be regrettable.

Case 15
A young couple were expecting their first baby and the wife was three months pregnant. She had been diagnosed as schizophrenic a year or so earlier; the husband was at 50 per cent risk of Huntington's disease, his mother being symptomatic. Because of their circumstances they were known to the social services. When the pregnancy was declared their social worker suggested it should be terminated, given the combination of medical problems. The husband was furious and the pregnancy went ahead. However, the mother had a psychotic episode later in the confinement and was judged unfit to look after the baby. For two years the father attempted to obtain custody of the baby but this was denied due to a combination of social problems and his risk of Huntington's. His sister offered to adopt the baby, and lived on the same housing estate, which would at least mean the father could see his child growing up.

However, the sister was denied the opportunity to adopt because she also, of course, was at the same risk of Huntington's. The baby was adopted elsewhere and 10 years later (when these events were related to a clinical geneticist) the father was very upset that he had no right to information about his child.

Comment
This case is related from the viewpoint of the birth father, who obviously feels aggrieved. The full details are not available, in particular the viewpoint of the social services. Nevertheless, the medical problems appear to have been a major factor in the difficult decision making. The case is unusual, not only because there were two medical problems with hereditary implications, but also because the birth *father* was so deeply involved prior to placement and is still experiencing the pain of events. From the clinical genetics standpoint the direct advice that the pregnancy be terminated is one that is no longer practised. Rather the approach is non-directive counselling which seeks to enable individuals and couples to make fully informed choices, and then to support the consultand(s) through that choice. Some of the pain experienced by this birth father may have been avoided if a more 'open' adoption placement had been made.

5 Adoption studies and the genetics of mental health and behaviour

Dr Peter Turnpenny and Dr Michael Morton

This chapter looks at the contribution that studies of adopted individuals have made, and continue to make, to the understanding of the heritability of certain mental illnesses, cognitive ability, and personality. The research methodology and main findings are summarised briefly, with some of the difficulties of such research illustrated by commenting on the studies of schizophrenia.

This book is principally concerned with the importance of genetic disease and heredity within the adoption process. This chapter acknowledges the significant contribution that adopted people, adoptive families, and adoption agencies have made to the understanding of genetics. At a time when the focus of excitement in genetics is concentrated on laboratory molecular science it is worth pausing to reflect on the contribution that adoption studies have made, and continue to make, to the understanding of heritability in the complex areas of mental health. Most common mental health disorders do not appear to be due to defects in single genes because family studies do not suggest a simple Mendelian pattern of inheritance with clearly defined genetic risk. The debate about the relative contributions of nature and nurture in the developing human psyche has a long history which predates modern genetic understanding. A nineteenth century literary study of nature and nurture in adoption is found in Wilkie Collins' novel *The Legacy of Cain.*[1]

Recent attempts to disentangle the influences of genetic and environmental factors have focused on the study of twins, adopted individuals and their families. This involves a view of adoption as a natural experiment, which can be examined in two ways. The first approach is to analyse the features of genetically unrelated individuals living together; this focuses on the importance of environmental influences within a family. The second approach, which has yielded more positive findings, concentrates on the features of genetically related individuals living apart in order to explore genetic influences on development. For both types of study it is essential to try and validate outcomes by incorporating appropriate matched control groups and comparing the findings.

A key concept in the examination of genetic influence is the idea of correlation or concordance figures, which is best explained in terms of twin studies. If identical (monozygotic – MZ) twins are reared apart, a study of a characteristic (or trait) which was found to be perfectly heritable with no environmental influence would reveal a correlation or concordance of 1.0. For non-identical (dizygotic – DZ) twins a similar trait would have a correlation of 0.5, assuming there were no environmental influences operating. The same correlation would be found between any first degree relatives for a purely heritable trait of this kind. A correlation of zero would suggest there was no heritability at all for the trait in question, the conclusion being that it was determined purely by environmental influences.

It can be seen that the study of MZ twins holds great interest, particularly those reared apart, possibly as a result of adoption. However, such twins are very rare and fewer than 100 MZ twin pairs have been studied in the world literature, although further studies currently underway will increase numbers considerably.[2] One of the problems of twin studies which arises in the area of adoption is the tendency of research to focus on conspicuous cases. Researchers in the past have become fascinated by the individual experience of small numbers of unusual twins, neglecting the possibility that there may be many other twin pairs where heritability of a trait is much less obvious. Research that focuses on the abnormal cases may produce falsely elevated correlations for heritability and possible ascertainment bias of this kind must be avoided by studying twins or adopted individuals in the context of the general population.

A profound difficulty for all research in the fields of psychology and psychiatry arises from questioning the validity and reliability of descriptive terminology, and therefore diagnostic labels. Thus, adoption studies which focus on the intelligence quotient (IQ) are criticised on the basis that IQ is a construct of limited validity in the prediction of individual attainment.[3] Similarly difficulties arise in adoption studies of mental illnesses where the diagnostic descriptions used within past research may be seen as unreliable in current psychiatric practice (see below).

Despite these constraints on the interpretation of adoption studies there is no doubt that findings from a careful examination of the process of adoption have contributed to the understanding of heritability of IQ,[4] alcoholism,[5] schizophrenia[6] and manic depression.[7] In the field of schizophrenia research an analysis of two classical adoption studies helps to clarify some of the critical issues.

Examples of adoption studies of schizophrenia
In 1966 Leonard Heston[8] published an influential paper examining the psychiatric disorders of 47 offspring of hospitalised schizophrenic mothers raised by non-schizophrenic carers and compared them with a matched group of 50 children with similar life histories whose biological mothers were not schizophrenic. Within this small sample it was found that the offspring of schizophrenic mothers had a significantly higher rate of schizophrenia than the control group. Higher rates of 'mental deficiency' and other disorders were found in these children and controversially the author attempted to combine varieties of psychiatric disorder, suggesting that the rate of transmission of disorder approached 50 per cent thereby implying a dominantly inherited single gene pattern. This study could be criticised as the genetic contribution from the fathers of the children was not taken into account. The key point from this study was that children of a schizophrenic mother have a higher than average risk of developing schizophrenia even when they are brought up away from the biological family. The finding that children with non-schizophrenic biological parents did not show this increased rate of schizophrenia addressed the criticism that there was a possibility that child care arrangements might predispose to mental disorder. The use of a control group meant that this study provided a strong argument for the existence of a genetic contribution to the development of schizophrenia.

A further critique of Heston's study concerns the issue of case selection; hospitalised schizophrenics may be an extremely disturbed subset of the population of sufferers from this condition. Some of the difficulties of Heston's study were resolved by the studies of Drs. Kety, Rosenthal, and colleagues,[9] which were based upon the production of an adoption register in Denmark that enabled schizophrenic adopted individuals to be identified within the context of the total population of adopted individuals in the country.

Whilst the work of Heston focused on adopted children of schizophrenic mothers, these studies explored the prevalence of schizophrenia and related disorders amongst the biological relatives of 33 adopted individuals who were identified as having schizophrenia, compared with a control group of adopted individuals with no psychiatric history. Biological relatives of subjects were compared with adoptive relatives and a significantly increased rate of schizophrenia-spectrum disorders was found in the former group.

A major criticism of the work of Rosenthal, Kety, and their colleagues, arose from a re-evaluation of the diagnosis of schizophrenia in the United States. The production of operationally defined research diagnostic criteria[10] led to greater clarity of definition of cases. Earlier studies were re-evaluated using such criteria and the boundaries of the schizophrenia spectrum were challenged. The wide ranging controversy about the value of the adoption research may be explored in the American Journal of Psychiatry.[11,12,13] Despite opposition amongst authors concerned about the implication of uncritical acceptance of genetic research,[14] there is no doubt that the study of adopted individuals provided powerful evidence supporting the proposal that schizophrenia is to some extent genetically determined.

Ongoing research

The scientific discipline of behavioural genetics is now well established[15,16] and the study of adopted individuals and their families, both biological and adoptive, continues to contribute to the understanding of genetic and environmental influences on many aspects of behaviour. Longitudinal studies offer new possibilities for developing understanding and the Colorado Adoption Project (CAP) is of particular interest. Commenced in 1975, CAP comprises 245 adoptive families and 245 matched non-adoptive families in which birth parents, adoptive parents, and the parents of non-adopted children have been administered a series of behavioural tests and measures. The children and their siblings, together with the home environments are studied annually from infancy through adolescence. Possible genetic influences on important aspects of personality, such as social competence, have been demonstrated using this methodology.[17]

An interesting shift in the understanding of the nature versus nurture debate in adoption arises from the realisation that parenting skills may themselves be influenced by genetic factors. Thus, in the language of one school of behavioural geneticists, the talk today is not so much about 'nature versus nurture', rather the focus is upon the 'nature of nurture'.[18]

References

1 Collins W, *The Legacy of Cain*, first published 1888, new edition 1993, Stroud, UK, publ. Allan Sutton.

2 Plomin R, DeFries J C, McClearn G E, *Behavioural Genetics: A primer*, 2nd Edn, W H Freeman & Co, 1990, USA.

3 Evans B, Waites B, *IQ and Mental Testing*, MacMillan, 1981.

4 Bouchard T J, McGue M, 'Familial studies of intelligence: a review' *Science*, 212: 1055-59, 1981.

5 Goodwin D W, Schulsinger F, Hermansen L, Guze S B, Winokur G, 'Alcohol problems in adoptees raised apart from alcoholic biological parents', *Arch Gen Psychiatry*, 28:238-49, 1973.

6 Murray R M, Revely A M, 'Genetic aspects of schizophrenia' *Contemporary Issues in Schizophrenia*, Eds. Kerr A, Snaith P, Gaskell (Roy Coll Psych), 1986.

7 Mendlewicz J, Rainer J D, 'Adoption study supporting genetic transmission in manic-depressive illness', *Nature*, 268:327-29, 1977.

8 Heston L L, 'Psychiatric disorders in foster home reared children of schizophrenic mothers', *British Journal of Psychiatry*, 112:819-25, 1966.

9 Kety S S, Rosenthal D, Wender P H, Schulsinger F, 'Mental illness in the biological and adoptive families of adopted schizophrenics', *American Journal of Psychiatry*, 128:302-06, 1971.

10 Spitzer R L, Endicott J, Robins E, 'Research diagnostic criteria, rationale and reliability', *Arch Gen Psychiat*, 35:773-82, 1978.

11 Lidz T, Blatt S, 'Critique of the Danish American studies of the biologic and adoptive relatives of adoptees who became schizophrenic', *American Journal of Psychiatry*, 140:426-35, 1983, USA.

12 Abrams R, Taylor M A, 'The genetics of schizophrenia: a reassessment using modern criteria', *American Journal of Psychiatry*, 140:171-75, 1983.

13 Kety S S, 'Mental illness in the biological and adoptive relatives of schizophrenic adoptees: findings relevant to genetic and environmental factors in etiology', *American Journal of Psychiatry*, 140:720-27, 1983, USA.

14 Rose S, Kamin L J, Lewaitin R C, *Not in our Genes*, Pelican, 1984.

15 Mann C, 'Behavioral genetics in transition', *Science*, 264:1686-89, 1994.

16 Plomin R, Owen M J, McGuffin P, 'The genetic basis of complex human behaviors', *Science*, 264:1733-39, 1994.

17 Plomin R, 'Nature, nurture and social development', *Social Development*, 3:37-53, 1994.

18 Plomin R, Bergeman C S, 'The nature of nurture: genetic influence on "environmental" measures', *Behavioral and Brain Sciences*, 14:373-427, 1991.

Section 2
What genetics can tell us

In the previous section the impact of genetics on adoption was described from the point of view of adoption practice. Mention was made of a variety of hereditary disorders without attempting to give a detailed explanation of either the diseases or their genetic basis. The purpose of the contributions in this section is to provide both the genetic basis of hereditary disease (Chapters 6 & 7) and to give an overview of some detailed medical applications (Chapters 8 – 10). The areas of medicine that have been selected are relatively common and likely to be increasingly relevant for the medical adviser whose task it is to assess the information available and make decisions about further enquiry and/or investigation. The content of these chapters is therefore most suitable for those with medical training and they help to convey some of the complexities that surround a particular diagnosis, hopefully shedding light on the implications and risks for family members. It is hoped that the content of both the basic science chapters and the applications will provide a useful resource for the areas covered, although developments are taking place so rapidly that up-to-date information will need to be sought for many conditions at the time they present a problem in adoption practice.

The section concludes with a contribution (Chapter 11) which describes the current directions of genetic research and the possible medico-social impact that developments will have on society, recognising that advances in genetic technology may pose difficult moral and legal dilemmas as well as providing us with some of the most dramatic and exciting breakthroughs in the history of medicine.

Chapter 6
Basic genetics, chromosomes, and Mendelian inheritance
Professor J A Raeburn

Chapter 7
Molecular genetics and the diagnosis of hereditary disease
Dr Kevin F Kelly

Chapter 8
Psychiatric, learning and behavioural disorders
Dr Sheila A Simpson

Chapter 9
Cancer genetics
Dr Deephti de Silva

Chapter 10
Congenital heart disease, adult cardiovascular disease and diabetes
Dr John C S Dean

Chapter 11
The future of genetics in medicine and society
Dr Neva Haites

6 Basic genetics, chromosomes, and Mendelian inheritance

Professor J A Raeburn

This chapter provides a useful introduction to the understanding of basic genetics. Starting with a problem-based approach, the chapter moves on to describe the main patterns of inheritance, and explains what is meant by single gene disorders, chromosome abnormalities, and multifactorial inheritance.

Historical background

Gregor Mendel, an Augustinian monk in Austria, described the principles of heredity in a paper published in 1865. He deduced from a study of peas that hereditary characters are transmitted from one generation to another as discrete units (later called genes). He also recognised the concepts of dominance and recessiveness. It was over three decades after Mendel's work, however, that doctors appreciated its relevance to human genetics. In 1906 Bateson coined the term "genetics" and in 1920 Garrod reported an inborn error of metabolism, alkaptonuria, the first human example of what is now referred to as Mendelian genetics.

In the 1930s Waardenberg theorised that Down's syndrome might be due to a chromosomal abnormality; it was not until 1959, however, that Lejeune and his colleagues in Paris showed that to be true and delineated the abnormality, trisomy 21. In the 1960s studies of chromosomes identified many other chromosome abnormality syndromes, most of them rare. In the 1970s and 1980s there was even more rapid progress; the era of molecular genetics was born and grew rapidly. The role of genetics in medicine continues to have an increasing impact, now including such common conditions as certain cancers and heart disorders.

Understanding basic genetics

The best way to understand basic genetics is to examine some situations in which a disease or characteristic affects a family and the

69

individuals within it and then to analyse the genetic explanation. It is useful to start with a brief account of how we begin to look at inheritance by preparing a family tree (pedigree). When studying the patterns produced by certain conditions we can find out if the disease occurs in just one generation or in several. We can see whether every affected person has an affected parent or if there is a tendency to skip generations.

Figure 1

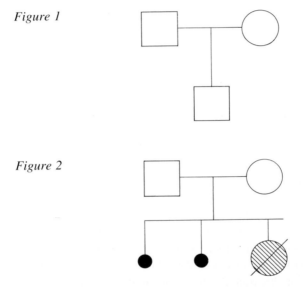

Figure 2

Figures 1 and 2 show some simple family structures from which we can build up our genetic understanding. Figure 1 shows a couple who have one son (males are shown as squares and females as circles). Figure 2 shows a couple with a more complex family tree. They have had three pregnancies; the first two miscarried, the third produced a baby girl who died. If the baby died prior to birth, it will be recorded as a stillbirth, often using the abbreviation SB.

Figure 3 takes this approach further and introduces an adoption situation. On the left of the drawing an unmarried couple (the dotted horizontal line between the parents of the boy indicates that they were not married) have decided to put forward the baby for adoption; the potential adoptive couple are shown on the right with their unfortunate obstetric history.

Figure 3

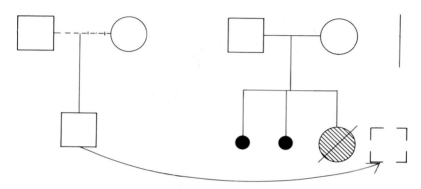

To understand the genetic basis of such family trees we need to know something about the cells which make up each organ and tissue of the body. Thus if we look at the skin or at the blood under the microscope we would see cells, characteristic of those tissues. Each cell will have a central darker staining part, the nucleus, which contains the hereditary material. During the process of cell division, nuclear material becomes less dense and it is then possible to see the rod-like structures called chromosomes, the name coming from the Greek for "coloured body". Chromosomes are a combination of nucleic acid and protein.

Genes, the units of genetic information, are encoded on the chromosomal DNA. Genes are sited in a linear order on chromosomes, each with its own defined site (or locus). Different species have their own characteristic chromosome pattern and number, known as the karyotype. In humans the chromosome number in every cell is 46, consisting of 23 pairs. Since we know that there are around 100,000 genes in the human it is clear that each chromosome has at least 1,000 genes located along its length. If we look now at Figure 4, a picture of the editor's own chromosomes(!), we see that changes in any part of a chromosome must involve many dozens, or even hundreds of genes.

Figure 4

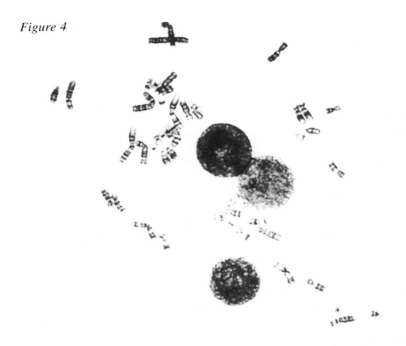

Next a brief introduction is needed to the main modes of inheritance. Table 1 shows the three major types of inheritance which have to be considered in order to understand the genetic issues concerning adoption. Conditions due to a single gene abnormality are caused by changes which affect functions of an individual gene and thus upset the synthesis of protein structures. Genetic changes (mutations) can occur in any functional part of a gene and may be a missing chemical sequence or possibly just one chemical substitution (see Chapter 7).

Table 1

Modes of inheritance

1. Single gene disorders
2. Chromosome disorders
3. Multifactorial disorders

Since each chromosome is a long sequence of DNA, with many genes along that length, chromosome disorders can obviously be major in their effect because they affect the normal working of several or many genes.

Multifactorial disorders involve several genes plus environmental factors and include relatively common conditions such as spina bifida, congenital heart disease, some types of diabetes and cleft lip and palate.

Single gene disorders
Each individual single gene disorder is usually quite rare, but cumulatively they account for a considerable amount of ill-health. To say to a family in which there are several affected people that the condition is rare would be to invite the response that "it is not rare with us"! Examples of single gene disorders are Duchenne muscular dystrophy, cystic fibrosis, Huntington's disease and familial polyposis coli. A table in the following chapter lists these and other rarer disorders along with brief notes on the systems affected and the type of inheritance.

At this point we will look at the patterns produced in families by the three types of single gene problem, including an indication of where in the adoption situation they may be encountered.

Table 2

Single gene disorders

---

1. Autosomal dominant
2. Autosomal recessive
3. Sex-linked disorders

Autosomal dominant disorders
In autosomal dominant disorders the usual pattern in the family is of affected individuals in each generation, the risk to the offspring of an affected person being 50 per cent that they will also inherit the abnormal gene. Figure 5 shows, on the left side, a family in which there is an autosomal dominant condition which has affected the grandfather and paternal uncle of the girl in generation III. If the girl's parents choose to place her for adoption, the history on the father's side

Figure 5

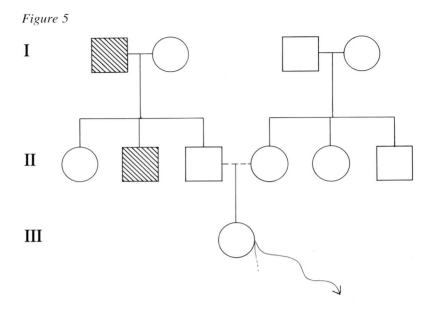

should be mentioned. If, for example, the condition was of late onset, such as Huntington's disease, and the girl's father was not yet at an age when the disease would be likely to manifest itself, then there is a significantly increased chance that the girl may have inherited the gene. Unless it can be shown that her birth father does not have the abnormal gene, she has a 25 per cent risk that she too may develop Huntington's disease.

An autosomal dominant condition is produced when one copy of an abnormal gene is able to disrupt normal gene function despite the normal gene on the corresponding location on the other chromosome of a pair (see Chapter 7). All normal people have two copies of all autosomes (ie. the non-sex chromosomes) and on those chromosomes the genes are also in pairs. If in a dominant disorder a person has one member of a gene pair affected then that is usually sufficient to cause the condition to be manifest at some stage in life. Not all autosomal dominants cause symptoms at birth however; some of them have quite late onset, even late in adult life.

Autosomal recessive disorders

The pattern in a family of an autosomal recessive disorder is quite different from that in autosomal dominance (Figure 6). As this figure shows the affected individuals (a boy and a girl) are both in one sibship (a group of full brothers and sisters). There are no people affected elsewhere in the pedigree; the parents of affected children in this family may rightly be puzzled that they have a genetic condition in their part of the family but there were "no warnings". The figure also shows a situation relevant to adoption.

Autosomal recessive conditions are caused when the affected person inherits an abnormal gene from *both* father and mother, thus having a double dose. In such situations the parents will both be carriers; in other words, they have one abnormal gene and one normal one at that genetic position. The answer to the question about why there has previously been no other affected person in the family is that carriers are always healthy; only when there are two copies of an abnormal gene, one from both parents, will there be an autosomal recessive disease. As the example shows (Figure 6), the high risk of being affected only occurs in the offspring of a couple who are both carriers.

The younger brother of the two affected individuals, having a girl friend who has become pregnant, may agree that adoption is the best arrangement. The social workers (and the prospective adoptive parents) may well wish reassurance that the problem in the third generation will not develop too in the adopted child. A knowledge of autosomal recessive inheritance can often lead to that reassurance. If a geneticist has confirmed the recessive nature of the condition in the two affected children, then the chance of the adoptive baby being at risk depends on the likelihood of the baby's mother and father both being carriers. If the disease were cystic fibrosis the father's chance of being a carrier is high (two chances out of three); however, the mother's chance of being a carrier is lower and in the UK the chance is about 1 in 25 (carrier frequencies for different disease genes vary according to ethnicity and race). Thus the overall chance that the baby in generation 4 has cystic fibrosis is 1 in 150 (2/3 – being the carrier risk to the sibling of the affected person – x 1/25 – being the general population risk of being a carrier – x 1/4 – being the risk of having an affected child if both parents are carriers). For cystic

Figure 6

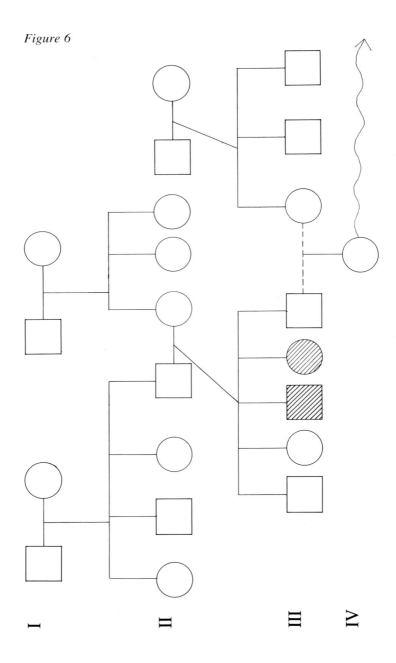

fibrosis it is possible to modify the chances by carrying out carrier testing in these types of situation.

Sex-linked disorders

The third type of single gene disorder is sex-linked inheritance where the abnormal gene is located on the X chromosome. All women have two copies of an X chromosome, having inherited one from each parent. Men have one copy of an X and one copy of the Y chromosome. Thus if a woman has an abnormality on one X chromosome she may not know this because she has an additional copy of the X which can compensate. Not so with men; if their single X chromosome is abnormal in one genetic site then they will show manifestations of the condition. An example, not unlikely to present in adoption situations, will illustrate what can happen.

In Figure 7, we see four generations of a family in which Duchenne muscular dystrophy has occurred, in generations II and III. The affected person in generation II died many years ago whilst the son with the condition in the third generation (aged 22) is very ill. If the 17-year-old younger sister of that ill young man becomes pregnant, the handling of any possible adoption of the son in the 4th generation would need to be especially sensitive but should involve making appropriate information available to possible adoptive parents. The adoptive parents may wish tests to be carried out on the boy in generation 4 to exclude Duchenne muscular dystrophy, but there is a difficult ethical issue to be considered in this situation.

The hypothetical situations (Figures 5, 6 and 7) illustrate that a genetic opinion should always be sought when there is a known (or possible) genetic disease in the biological family of the child being adopted.

Chromosome disorders

Conditions which are chromosomal involve either the whole or part of a chromosome. Each chromosome exists as a member of a pair, with one copy being inherited from each parent. Thus we each have two copies of chromosome number one, two of chromosome two, and so on. Examination of the chromosomes of a pair individually, using a microscope, will not make it possible to identify from which parent one

Figure 7

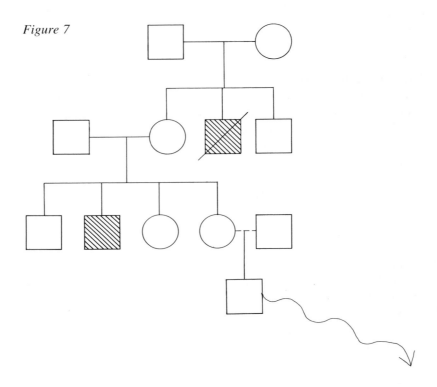

or other chromosome came. The only exceptions to this are:

a) the sex chromosomes, X and Y, in which females have two copies of the X chromosome and men have one X, and one Y (see above) and

b) those few chromosomes which have unusual patterns which can be distinguished in several members of a family, the patterns being inherited in a single gene manner.

As mentioned earlier, disorders of chromosomes involve either an extra (or a missing) copy of a chromosome and thus there is imbalance of a number of genes, not just of one. Because of this, chromosome disorders are usually severe in their manifestations, with marked learning difficulty, a variety of congenital abnormalities and usually a very poor prognosis. Chromosome disorders are often recognised at birth and therefore a possible chromosomal problem will usually have been identified before adoption. Down's syndrome is the most common and a condition in which there is already considerable experience of successful adoption placements.

Multifactorial disorders

With these genetic conditions the cause of abnormality is a combination of genetic and environmental factors. Manipulation of the environment may be possible, for example, the taking of folic acid around the time of conception has been shown to reduce the incidence of spina bifida. In general, the risk of a further multifactorial disorder occurring in a family with one affected person is going to be low. Therefore the potential adoption of a child, one of whose biological parents had a family history of clefting of the palate, for example, is unlikely to be compromised. However, because there is often much anxiety in the adoptive parents about genetic diseases, accurate information should be sought and usually a geneticist's opinion will be useful.

General aspects

From an adoption viewpoint some genetic disorders may already be known about prior to embarking on the matching and selection process. However, it is hoped that a detailed medical history of the first and second degree relatives (ie. the offspring, siblings and parents) of the birth parents will be obtained. This is important for the future of the adopted person, the adoptive parents, and in some cases, for the birth parents and the wider family.

7 Molecular genetics and the diagnosis of hereditary disease

Dr Kevin F Kelly

This chapter outlines some of the basic principles of molecular genetics and describes some of the kinds of mutation now known to cause genetic disease. The single gene disorders discussed include cystic fibrosis and Fragile X mental retardation, and the author provides useful information on the detection of genetic mutation.

For many years, carriers of the cystic fibrosis gene were only identified when an affected child was born to a carrier couple. In other genetic conditions, clinical signs could indicate the presence of a disease but predicting which child of an affected parent had inherited the disorder was often difficult until symptoms developed. A fairly successful technique known as linkage analysis was developed for tracking genes in families and this method could be applied to disorders like Huntington's disease and myotonic dystrophy. The technique had significant disadvantages as family structures were required for the method to work and often the analyses proved to be uninformative.

Linkage analysis is a method of following the inheritance of a marker (in this case a disease gene), the exact nature of which is unknown, by following the inheritance of another marker which can be identified and which is apparently linked to the disease. The inheritance of myotonic dystrophy in families was followed by looking at certain blood group factors. Although linkage analysis is a useful method, for various reasons it does not always work.

Advances in molecular biology have, for the first time, offered the possibility that for significant genetic diseases carrier status can be determined or presymptomatic testing carried out in the absence of known family histories of disease. The following sections provide some of the background in molecular biology necessary to understand genetic testing and its limitations.

The processes whereby an organism replicates itself are intricate, comprising of an interrelated progression of events with each step depending on the correct completion of an earlier step, and so on. When mistakes occur in these steps the organism may suffer if the error is severe enough. Sometimes, an error may be transmitted to the offspring where the disorder occurs again and in this way genetic disease proceeds through the generations. In order to understand a little of the complexity of cell function and how errors can lead to genetic disease, there follows a brief description of some of the basic principles of molecular genetics.

DNA structure

In the 1940s, analysis of genetic material was underway. It was shown that by adding deoxyribonucleic acid (DNA) from one bacterial strain to another, heritable characteristics were also transferred. DNA is found in the nucleus of the cell, which is the basic unit of construction of organs and tissues. In 1953, Watson and Crick described the molecular structure of DNA. DNA is composed of bases (see below) linked together and the order of the bases in groups of three make up the codes for the amino acid sequence in proteins. By the mid 1950s the study of human chromosomes produced significant findings about normal and abnormal chromosome structure. In the last 20 years there has been a vast expansion in molecular genetics research leading to the Human Genome Project which has the aim of decoding the entire human genome.

DNA is a polymer, or chain of units known as nucleotides, linked together in a linear fashion. There are four chemicals or nucleotide bases, Adenine (A), Guanine (G), Thymine (T), and Cytosine (C). The nucleotides are complex structures made up of a nitrogen containing base linked to a 5-carbon sugar unit, and each base is linked to the next by means of a phosphate group. The base, sugar and phosphate unit together form the nucleotide. Early X-ray diffraction studies suggested that DNA consisted of two strands wound together in a helical form. A model for the structure of DNA which explained the X-ray diffraction appearances was proposed by Watson and Crick in 1953. In this model, the two strands of DNA formed a spiral staircase-like structure held together by hydrogen bonds between the bases (see Figure 1).

Figure 1 **DNA structure**

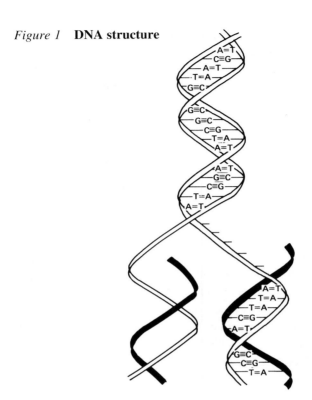

The four bases can be in any order along the chains but if the two sides of the 'staircase' are examined it will be seen that base G always pairs with base C, and A always pairs with T (complementary base pairing). Thus, if the base order in one strand is known then the base order in the other can be deduced.

Watson and Crick suggested how the double stranded structure could explain DNA replication. If two strands were to separate, each strand would form a template on which another strand could be formed producing an exact copy of the original.

Human cells contain about 7×10^9 base pairs (bp) of DNA with sperm and egg cells containing about half that amount. Since genetic information is coded in the order of the bases in DNA, each cell potentially carries a huge amount of genetic information.

Genes

Genes are the units of information distributed along the length of the chromosome (see Chapter 6). The evidence that DNA is the substance of which chromosomes and genes are made came as long ago as 1944 when it was shown that the addition of purified DNA from one bacterial strain to another also transferred characteristics of the donor cells to the recipients. Genes contain the information for the production of proteins coded in the sequence of nucleotide bases which make up the gene. Unravelling the process by which the information contained in the genes in coded form is transformed into working protein molecules and cell structures has been one of the great scientific advances of the 20th century. This process is known as 'transcription' and 'translation' (see Figures 2-4).

Information is converted from DNA code to protein structure by means of an intermediate structure called messenger ribonucleic acid (mRNA). RNA is a similar structure to DNA with some differences. This information pathway of DNA directing the sequence and production of RNA which in turn directs the sequence and production of protein is known today as the 'central dogma' of molecular biology.

Errors can occur at many stages in the mechanisms described although cells possess many repair processes which ensure that errors are corrected before the organism suffers damage. When an error does occur, ie. a mutation, genetic disease may be the result. The process outlined is, in fact, extremely complex and, like all complex processes, may go wrong.

Genetic disease

The diseases considered here are single gene disorders where disease results from a defect in one gene and such disorders can be autosomal dominant, for example, Huntington's disease, where inheritance of an affected gene means that an individual will develop the disease. In autosomal recessive conditions, such as cystic fibrosis, an individual may be a carrier of the gene mutation with no ill effects. If a child is unfortunate enough to inherit two faulty genes from its carrier parents

Figure 2 **Transcription**

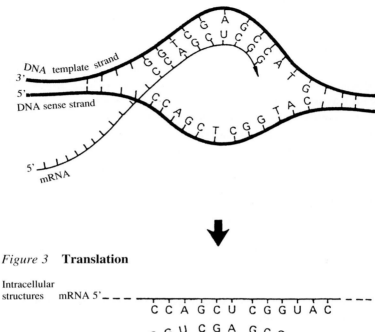

Figure 3 **Translation**

Intracellular
structures   mRNA 5'

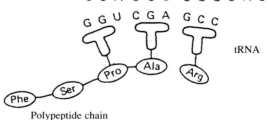

Polypeptide chain

Process of transcription and translation

When the process of 'reading' a gene is initiated the two DNA strands separate and a complementary strand of 'messenger RNA' (mRNA, which differs slightly from DNA) is formed (a) The mRNA strand is now the new template along which each sequence of 3 bases is recognised by another chemical called transfer RNA (tRNA) (b) the tRNA molecules carry specific amino acids which then join together to form a protein chain. This part of the process takes place in "ribosomes" which are sub-microscopic (see Figure 4).

Figure 4

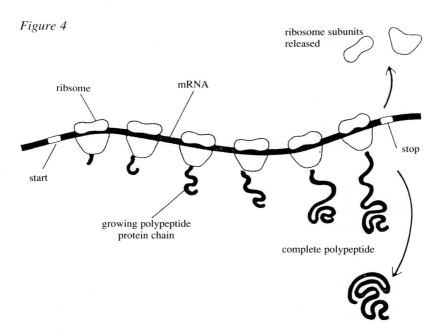

then it will be affected by the disease. Sex-linked conditions, such as Duchenne muscular dystrophy or haemophilia, are caused by errors on the X chromosome; females are carriers of these conditions and males are affected. By 1990 over 3,000 single gene disorders had been described and the number is rising continually.

Genetic disease originates from a number of different kinds of mutations affecting DNA and through the information pathway described above, the protein products of the cell. Some genetic diseases familiar to clinicians in the UK will be considered and Table 1 below shows the frequency per 1,000 births for various single gene disorders in Northern Europe. It is mainly disorders like these which will be of importance when attempting to determine the genetic history of children for adoption. For a number of genetic disorders, molecular screening techniques are already available and the ethical problems of how the methodologies should be used are becoming apparent. The next sections describe the operation of some mutation tests currently available using as examples cystic fibrosis and Fragile X mental retardation.

Table 1

Inherited disorders in Northern Europe

	Type	*Frequency/1,000 births*
Huntington's disease	AD	0.20
Myotonic dystrophy	AD	0.25
Polycystic kidney disease	AD	1.00
Cystic fibrosis	AR	0.50
Phenylketonuria	AR	0.20 – 0.50
Duchenne muscular dystrophy	XL	0.30
Haemophilia	XL	0.10
Fragile X mental retardation	XL	0.90

AD – Autosomal Dominant
AR – Autosomal Recessive
XL – X-Linked

Cystic fibrosis

In the UK, cystic fibrosis is the commonest serious autosomal recessive condition with a frequency of about 1 per 2,500 births. The gene for this condition, which is located on chromosome 7, was identified in 1989 and with it the mutation which is responsible for most of the cystic fibrosis in the UK. This mutation consists of three missing bases (a deletion). This means that the structure of the protein coded for by the whole gene is defective due to the loss of one amino acid. The defective protein does not work as it should. An individual who has a defective copy of the gene on one chromosome but a normal copy on the other chromosome is called a carrier. Carriers can survive perfectly well with only one normal gene. If a carrier female and a carrier male produce a child who inherits both defective genes then that child is affected by the disease cystic fibrosis.

Molecular testing is currently available which allows the detection of 80-90 per cent of the common cystic fibrosis mutations in the UK population. The test is relatively simple to perform and can be carried out on mouthwash samples, eliminating the need for blood taking.

Mutation detection

How is the mutation detected? Mutation detection in cystic fibrosis, and indeed many genetic diseases, employs the powerful technique of DNA amplification also called the Polymerase Chain Reaction or PCR. DNA amplification produces many copies of the damaged region of a gene by using specific primers which target the region of interest. The amplified region can then be examined by analytical techniques which might, for example, measure the size of the target region in comparison to a normal region. In the case of the common cystic fibrosis mutation known as 'delta F508', the normal target region would be 100 bases long but if three bases were missing then the target would be 97 bases long. Since we possess two copies of each chromosome then a carrier of cystic fibrosis would show one target of 100 bases and one of 97 bases, a normal individual would have two targets of 100 bases while a person affected by cystic fibrosis would have two targets of 97 bases. Figure 5 shows a representation of a PCR mutation analysis.

The diagram (Figure 5) represents a PCR analysis of the delta F508 mutation. Individuals 1 and 2 are the cystic fibrosis carrier parents of child 3 who is affected. The PCR products are separated by gel electrophoresis, stained and photographed. The parents 1 and 2 each have a fragment of 100 bases and 97 bases. The child (3) has inherited a 97 base fragment from each parent; this represents two damaged genes so the child is affected by cystic fibrosis.

A number of other mutation detection procedures are currently available which will detect up to 90 per cent of the cystic fibrosis mutations in the British population. Mutation tests can be carried out for other genetic diseases, for example, Fragile X mental retardation, Huntington's disease, Duchenne muscular dystrophy and myotonic dystrophy. These tests may involve PCR as described for cystic fibrosis or a technique called Southern analysis (after its inventor Professor E Southern) in the case of myotonic dystrophy or Fragile X mental retardation.

Southern analysis

It is not uncommon for a genetic disease to be caused by a mutation which increases the size of a particular important region of a gene in some uncontrolled way. Some examples of this kind of mutation are described

Figure 5 **Analysis of CF mutation**

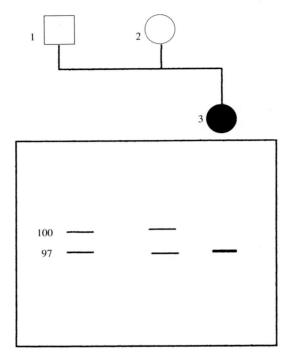

in the section on trinucleotide repeats. Alterations in the size of DNA fragments can be detected by the technique of Southern analysis (or 'blotting'). The process is summarised in Figure 6.

Human DNA can easily be extracted from a blood sample, or in the case of a prenatal diagnosis, chorion villus or amniocytes. The purified DNA is then broken up into small fragments by special enzymes called restriction enzymes. The resulting mixture of DNA fragments is then separated according to size in a procedure known as gel electrophoresis. A tiny sample of the cut DNA is added to a small well in a slab of agarose gel and an electric current applied. The smallest fragments move most quickly through the gel while larger fragments move more slowly (Fig 6a). Among all of this DNA are the targets of interest, the pieces of DNA from the disease gene and they must be found in some way. The gels themselves are too

Figure 6 **Southern blotting**

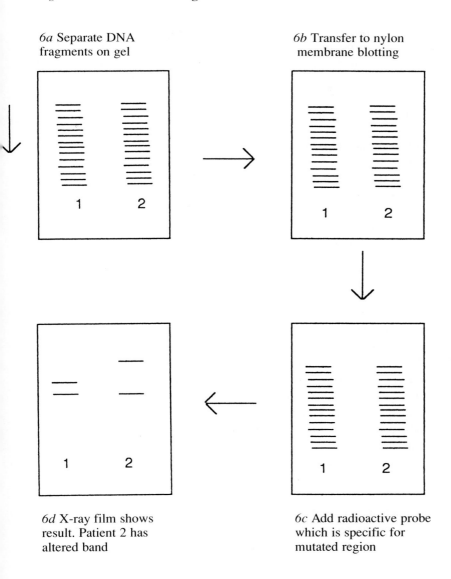

6a Separate DNA
fragments on gel

6b Transfer to nylon
membrane blotting

6d X-ray film shows
result. Patient 2 has
altered band

6c Add radioactive probe
which is specific for
mutated region

fragile to test so the DNA contained in them is transferred to tough nylon paper in a process akin to blotting an ink stain to form an exact replica of the original gel (Fig 6b). The nylon blot is then soaked in a radioactive probe which is specific for the gene of interest and can pick it out from all of the other DNA present (Fig 6c). An X-ray film is placed over the nylon and two or three days later, the resulting image developed (Fig 6d). In Fig 6d, patient 1 has two bands close together while patient 2 has one band which is increased in size due to the presence of a mutation.

Fragile X mental retardation

With a frequency of 0.9 per 1,000 males, Fragile X mental retardation is the commonest inherited form of mental retardation and is second only to Down's syndrome as a cause of mental retardation in males. The name refers to an area on the X chromosome called a fragile site which may often be detected by staining chromosomes and examining them under the microscope. Under certain culture conditions, the X chromosome of the Fragile X patient appears under the microscope to contain a gap. This is not always a certain diagnostic test since fragile sites may sometimes not be detected even in the presence of the disorder.

Fragile X syndrome is interesting in other ways, since it can be transmitted by normal males who carry a 'premutation'. Normal transmitting males never have affected daughters but their grandchildren of both sexes may be affected. This observation gave rise to the idea that the premutation converts to a full mutation causing the disorder after passing through a female meiosis. In 1991, a gene was identified which is now believed to be the cause of the majority of Fragile X mental retardation. The gene has been called FMR 1 and a study of its structure has helped explain many of the puzzling features of the disorder. The gene was found to contain a region of unstable DNA in the form of a peculiar feature called a trinucleotide repeat, a feature since discovered in the genes for Huntington's disease and myotonic dystrophy.

Trinucleotide repeats

Trinucleotide repeats are regions of DNA where there is a pattern of identical triplets of bases repeated from 3 to >2,000 times, for instance, CTGCTGCTGCTG . . . Other trinucleotide repeat examples are shown in Table 2. Trinucleotide repeat regions have been found associated with genes in a number of disorders where they may display a high degree of instability. For the disorders in question there appears to be a 'normal' range in the number of repeats but if this number is exceeded the result is expression of the genetic disease. It may be the case that mutation events occur in normal chromosomes with higher numbers of repeats and this causes the repeat to become unstable. It is believed that once a mutation has expanded beyond a certain limit, the information pathway from DNA to protein is disturbed. Expansions may cause the production of a faulty protein, or, if the expansion is in a control region, the quantity of protein produced might be affected.

As the unstable mutation is transmitted through the generations it can expand from a comparatively innocuous 'premutation' and lead to an increase in the severity of the disease, an effect seen in myotonic dystrophy or in Fragile X. In these disorders, a mother carrying a 'premutation' expansion can have an affected child where the repeat number may be multiplied ten-fold above the normal upper limit. The normal ranges and expansion sizes for five of the genetic diseases where a trinucleotide repeat mutation occurs are shown in Table 2.

Table 2

Genetic diseases where expansion of a trinucleotide repeat is involved

Disorder	Repeat	Normal Range	Expansion Range
Myotonic dystrophy	CTG	3-37	35->2000
Huntington's disease	CAG	6-37	36-121
Kennedy disease	CAG	11-33	40-62
Fragile X syndrome	CGG	7-52	50->2000
Spinocerebellar ataxia (I)	CAG	19-36	43-81

The important point to be noted is that for significant genetic disorders, mutations with causal involvement in the manifestation of the diseases have been identified. Application of PCR-based analytical techniques or DNA probing methodology allows the identification or exclusion of mutations in 'at risk' individuals. In some conditions such as familial bowel cancer, there may be too many mutations to detect by a simple procedure, or in other cases, the gene may not yet be identified. In cases like these a process known as gene tracking may be employed providing there are enough family members available and markers close to the gene have been identified.

Gene tracking

This technique depends on the presence of some marker close to the gene of interest which can be easily detected. One such marker is a region of DNA which differs in size between individual chromosomes. These regions known as polymorphisms are common on all chromosomes and are often found close enough to genes to act as markers. The process of analysis of polymorphisms involves Southern blotting as described earlier. The chromosome markers (polymorphisms) are DNA fragments of different sizes and these fragments can be identified by Southern blotting. Figure 7 shows how the procedure works.

The diagram shows a family affected by a genetic disease; members who have the disease are shown as closed symbols. The wife of affected son (II-3) is pregnant and requests an exclusion test for her unborn baby, III-1. A family analysis is carried out since the gene for the disease has not yet been found but a polymorphic marker for the gene is available. The marker sizes are determined by Southern analysis. Inheritance of the chromosome in question can now be followed through the family. The affected grandmother in this family (I-1) has markers 1 and 5 while her husband (I-2) has markers 2 and 3. Both affected children have inherited marker 1 from their mother while the unaffected son (II-2) has inherited marker 5 from his mother. It appears as if marker 1 (in box) is linked to the disease. If the child of II-3 and II-4 inherits marker 1 from its father, the child too will be at risk from the disease but if as in the case shown the child inherits marker 2 from its father, the child will probably be unaffected. Marker 2 originates with the baby's grandfather (I-2). The main disadvantage of this technique is that it cannot be carried out unless a family structure is available.

Conclusion

This chapter has outlined some of the basic principles of molecular genetics and described some of the kinds of mutation now known to cause genetic disease. For the disorders discussed, and for others such as

Figure 7 **Gene tracking**

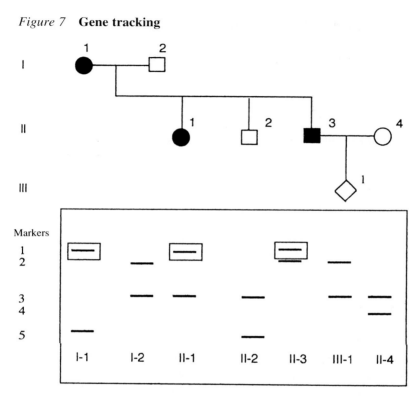

haemophilia and Duchenne muscular dystrophy, mutation screening tests are available which could be used to identify carriers of the disorder. It seems, however, that in considering the adoption process the most important factor would be to obtain as accurate a medical history as possible from the mother of the child involved. In the absence of an accurate history it would be difficult to decide what tests, if any, could be employed. It would not seem reasonable to test for everything for which there is a test available. Where the gene is not known and a direct mutation test not possible, tracking procedures may be the only option left. Gene tracking requires a family structure often not available, especially in the adoption situation. The technology exists to offer screening for mutations but the questions which remain to be answered are how and when the technology should be applied.

8   Psychiatric, learning and behavioural disorders

Dr Sheila A Simpson

Psychiatric and learning disorders give rise to some of the most difficult and contentious decision making in the whole of adoption practice. Adverse mental health and/or poor parenting may be the cause of relinquishment of young children and the relative influences of heredity and upbringing might then be debated for the long-term outcome for the child who is to be fostered or adopted. These difficult cases are in part a reflection of our poor understanding of the factors which contribute to 'normal' mental health. However, much progress has been made in defining some relatively common disorders which have a genetic basis, and this chapter provides an overview of these conditions, as well as others which are not yielding their secrets so easily.

Psychiatric disorders

Many common psychiatric disorders arise in childhood and little is known about their aetiology, although an increasing number of psychiatric and learning disorders can be said to have a genetic component.[1] The advent of the science of molecular genetics has enabled significant advances to be made in the accurate diagnosis and prediction of some of these disorders, but there have proved to be many problems in the use of this new technology. One of the principal reasons for this is the difficulty of accurate diagnosis of the problem to be investigated. Psychiatric diagnoses are rarely supported by objective laboratory tests, and, in the context of genetic research, the stigmata of these disorders makes family studies extremely difficult.

The debate over the relative contribution of nature and nurture has long raged. 'Nature' in this context means genetic make-up, but it is clear that personality, behaviour, and frank mental illness can all be affected and influenced by upbringing or 'nurture'. Environmental factors must be considered in any family where psychiatric disease appears. Poor social circumstances, psychiatric disease in a parent, or dysfunctional parenting may all contribute to the mental ill health of a young person. Abuse in childhood, whether it be physical, sexual or psychological has long-term effects upon the developing child, even after successful placement. These are not truly 'genetic', but certainly relate to the child's early environment.

Psychoses

Psychoses are psychiatric disorders that are characterised by the loss of ability to tell the difference between external reality and experiences within the self. Some psychoses are described as organic since it is clear that they arise from demonstrable structural disease of the brain, such as brain tumours or degeneration. These can occur in old age, or in childhood, and an increasing number have a recognised genetic basis.

Alzheimer's disease

This is the most common form of senile dementia, and over 750,000 people in the UK are affected. It principally affects individuals in late middle age and beyond. Characteristic plaques containing Beta amyloid protein appear in parts of the the brain which are involved in memory and cognition. Familial Alzheimer's disease is rare, but early onset familial Alzheimer's (earlier than 65 years of age) can be transmitted as an autosomal dominant trait. Mutations in the amyloid precursor protein on chromosome 21 have been demonstrated[2] and the inheritance of one of these mutations completely predicts the inheritance of the disease. An additional locus on chromosome 14[3] has been identified and the combined data suggest that the genetic sites accounting for most early onset familial Alzheimer's disease have now been found.

The much more common senile, sporadic form of this disease is far less well understood. There is an association of one of the apolipoprotein E alleles (e4) to familial and sporadic Alzheimer's disease. This polymorphic protein has a central role in the metabolism of cholesterol and triglycerides, and the presence of the e4 allele in the heterozygous or homozygous state significantly increases the risk of developing Alzheimer's disease.[4]

Pick disease

This type of dementia is much less common than Alzheimer's, but there are many similarities in the clinical features. Diagnosis is often made after death when the characteristic pathological findings have been seen. Families with autosomal dominant inheritance are described [5,6] but there is debate about the mode of transmission of this disorder.

Huntington's disease

This neurodegenerative disease is less common than Alzheimer's disease. About 6,000 people in the UK are affected, but its effects are none the less devastating. It is an autosomal dominant disease (and therefore affects both sexes equally) and is fully penetrant; most individuals are affected by their early 40s, and most have had children before the diagnosis is made. There is well documented evidence of the morbidity associated with being a Huntington's family member.

Affected individuals have a movement disorder which is choreiform in nature, personality changes occur, and psychiatric disease such as psychoses and neuroses are commonly found, as well as severe cognitive deficit. Death occurs usually within 20 years from onset of signs. The disease is often misdiagnosed or hidden within families, although since March 1993[7] it has been possible to identify the mutation on chromosome 4 uniquely associated with the disease. This can be accomplished by means of a single blood sample, either to confirm a diagnosis made clinically or to predict status in an individual at risk (after adequate counselling and preparation).

Onset in childhood is recognised, and accounts for between 3-10 per cent of all cases. It is more common if the father was the affected parent. Chorea is usually less marked, but mental deterioration is severe. Epilepsy is a common feature, and decline is generally rapid.

There have been many studies of the affects of predictive testing in this disease group.[8] Problems with insurance, employment and personal relationships can occur; the decision to undergo such testing is not to be taken lightly. Screening of children (under the age of eighteen) does not have the support of clinical geneticists in the UK.[9]

Schizophrenia

There is evidence to suggest that this disorder can be included among those which are linked to structural changes within the brain.[10] The personal, social and economic consequences of this disorder make it one of the most serious of the psychiatric disorders as well as being a significant public health problem. There is a large body of literature, much of it conflicting, which has failed to clarify the pathophysiology of schizophrenia. The neurodevelopmental hypothesis contends that in foetal or immediate postnatal life the establishment of fundamental aspects of cerebral structure and function is subtly but critically disrupted.[11] D3 and D4 dopamine receptors in the limbic system appear to have a key role and studies have indicated that the abnormal regulation of these receptors may be involved in the aetiology of this disorder.[12]

A gene for schizophrenia has not yet been defined and research into the genetic basis of schizophrenia has been fraught with difficulty[13] because of the varying clinical picture this disease may present, even in one family. Misdiagnosis is common, and some families undoubtedly have more than one case of psychiatric disease by tragic coincidence only, rather than because there is a genetic trait segregating in the family.

The evaluation of risk is not wholly dependent on mutation analysis. By studying the family history of an individual it is possible to assess the likelihood of that person developing the family disorder, based on recognised patterns of inheritance. In this context there are a very few families where schizophrenia appears to be inherited in an autosomal dominant fashion, with risks to offspring as high as 50 per cent. On the other hand, even these families show incomplete penetrance, where the disease may appear to skip a generation, or appear in a modified form.

The population risk of developing schizophrenia is nearly one per cent, but numerous studies, which have included tracing adopted children (see Chapter 5), have shown that there is a familial tendency. The risks to family members are modified by the type of schizophrenia in the relative, that is, whether it is mild and late onset (where risk is relatively less), or of the hebephrenic or catatonic type (where there is an increased risk). An approximate risk to offspring of someone with the disorder is 13 per cent, or 9 per cent if a brother or sister is affected rather than a parent.[14] There is also an increased frequency of other, specific psychiatric states in relatives of those who suffer from schizophrenia. Caution is urged in the use of these figures when giving advice to families where accurate family history information is not available, and where the diagnosis may not be reliable.

Affective disorders

These disorders are so called because one of their main features is abnormality of mood, characterised by episodes of dysphoria that can be associated with somatic symptoms. Many levels of mood disorder exist, and depressive symptoms are common in the general population, but genetic factors are best described in the major unipolar (purely depressive) and bipolar (manic depressive) disorders. The role of genetic factors is indicated by concordance in monozygotic (57 per cent) and dizygotic twins (14 per cent), and the correlation between adopted persons and their biologic relatives.[15]

The lifetime risk of developing a major manic depressive psychosis is about one percent, but as high as 5 per cent if milder forms are included. Like schizophrenia, the risks to relatives are higher if the onset of the disorder is at a younger age. Greatly varying risks are given by various authors, but the risks to first degree relatives (sibling, offspring) of developing an affective psychosis could be as high as 20 per cent if age of onset was below 40 years of age, but about 10 per cent if age of onset was above 40 years.

A susceptibility gene in the pericentromeric region of chromosome 18 has been postulated, with a complex mode of inheritance.[16] Linkage to chromosome 21 and X linked inheritance has also been suggested, and there is therefore much debate.[17,18] These hypotheses are not mutually exclusive, since both X linked and autosomal genes may collaborate and there may be genetic heterogeneity.

Other psychiatric or behavioural disorders

These disorders have been the cause of much debate in the scientific community. The relative importance of environment and heredity, and the classification and aetiology are much less certain. A variety of conditions such as anxiety neuroses and personality traits have been the subject of family study by scientists, clinicians and the media, but there are no clear cut data which a geneticist could use to predict their occurrence within the family. The problems described are frequent in the community, and the range of normality is wide. There may well be subgroups amongst these problems, such as alcoholism, where it is possible that there may be genetically inherited forms of enzyme deficiency which predispose an individual to developing such a disorder, but there is no clear evidence upon which to give advice to prospective adoptive parents.

The XYY syndrome

This problem occurs when an additional Y chromosome is present in the male child and has a frequency of 1.5/1,000 live births. The boy may be of increased height, and may be more prone to acne. It has been suggested[19] that these children were of lower IQ than average, and that aneuploidy (an abnormal number of chromosomes in the cells) may cause impairment of neurologic maturation, and minimal brain dysfunction.

Early studies on the genetic basis of criminality amongst the prison population appeared to show that there was a higher than expected number of XYY males. However, recent, well controlled, prospective studies, have refuted the association of criminal behaviour with this karyotype. It seems that the great majority of XYY men function normally in society.[20] The fertility of these men is normal, and there is no evidence that their own children are at risk of being chromosomally abnormal.

Neurofibromatosis

There are two distinct types of this neurocutaneous disorder, as has been proven by the finding of two responsible genes, neurofibromatosis type 1 (NF1) on chromosome 17, and NF2 on chromosome 22. NF1 affects tissues derived from neural crest cells, and the clinical features are very variable; cafe au lait spots, skin neurofibromas and Lisch nodules of the iris are diagnostic. It has an incidence of about 1 in 3,000. NF2 is less common (about 1 in 37,000) and predisposes individuals to develop tumours of the central nervous system.[21]

Both disorders are inherited as autosomal dominant traits, but any one of many different mutations in the gene may be responsible and it is not feasible to screen individuals as yet. In addition, about half of all cases are the result of a new mutation in the affected individual when the offspring of the affected individual are at 50 per cent risk of developing the disorder, but not their siblings.

This disorder is included here because well recognised behaviour and learning difficulties commonly occur. Non verbal learning difficulties are present in about one third of all NF children, and each child requires careful assessment to help them achieve their full potential. Classically the child may have an attention deficit, exhibit motor clumsiness, have visuospatial difficulties, and may have been diagnosed as being autistic or even depressed as a result of their social isolation. Assessment should include educational and psychological evaluation, as well as testing of their motor co-ordination. A detailed clinical examination is necessary to make the diagnosis in any child where a family history of the disease exists, or where clinical suspicion arises.

There is a very active patient support group for this condition, and much useful information about management and current research is available on request.

The Tourette syndrome (or Gilles de la Tourette syndrome)
This disorder is characterised by childhood onset of motor and vocal tics, often with behavioural problems. Tourette syndrome can be distressing for the families and friends of the affected individual, since the vocal tics can be in the form of foul language which the sufferer is unable to control. It has been over diagnosed in some areas (notably the USA) and may well not be diagnosed sufficiently in the UK. It can run a fluctuating course in childhood.

Seventy five per cent of patients are male, with the onset of symptoms between the ages of 2 and 14 years; 10 per cent of cases have a family history. Pauls[22] found an increased frequency of obsessive compulsive disorder and the Tourette syndrome in first degree relatives. Families are described where autism or pervasive developmental disorder coexisted with Tourette's syndrome. The genetics are poorly understood and if a major single gene is responsible, it has not been identified. In 1990, Comings[23] suggested tryptophan oxygenase as a possible candidate gene. Another author[24] described the gene as autosomal dominant with incomplete penetrance, and variable expression.

Autism

The frequency of autism is said to be about 4-6/10,000[25] but it may be over diagnosed. It is characteristically diagnosed in a child who is uncommunicative and unable to make warm emotional relationships with people. These children avoid eye contact, have learning problems (especially in speech) and behaviour difficulties. Over 75 per cent of autistic children are clearly developmentally delayed. Individuals with autistic symptoms without the full clinical picture may be regarded as having Asperger's syndrome, and there is no clear evidence as yet for a genetic basis for that disorder.

A few specific disease entities are associated with autism, some of which are genetic. The most notable is the Fragile X syndrome (see below). About five per cent of all autism cases may have tuberous sclerosis, and associated infantile spasms.[26] This neurocutaneous malformation is characterised by mental retardation, epileptic seizures, adenoma sebaceum, subungual fibromata and a variety of rare tumours. It is an autosomal dominant disorder, and therefore offspring of affected individuals are at 50 per cent risk of developing it. A large proportion of cases are due to new mutations where there is no family history, but a risk to sibs of the index case remains since one of the parents may be a gonadal mosaic for the gene fault.

A number of metabolic disorders are associated with autism, such as disorders of purine metabolism and phenylketonuria. Most of these disorders are inherited in a recessive manner with a 1 in 4 risk to offspring in each pregnancy of carriers. These carriers are healthy and asymptomatic, and only at risk of producing affected children if they partner another carrier of the disorder. The risk of partnering a carrier is small, unless the couple are related.

About 10-20 per cent of children with autism show improvement in their signs at about the age of 4-6 years and go on to attend ordinary school and obtain employment.[27] Autistic individuals rarely marry and have children, and there are no cases of affected individuals with affected parents.[28] The risk to siblings is small but significant (about two per cent).

Porphyria

The inherited porphyrias are a diverse group of metabolic disorders which can be inherited in an autosomal dominant or recessive manner. The major clinical manifestations result from the accumulation of porphyrin precursors or porphyrins which cause neurological symptoms or cutaneous photosensitivity. The clinical exacerbation and severity of the disorders are partly determined by environmental and metabolic factors such as drugs and hormones. Recognition of the diagnosis can lead to reduced morbidity in this patient group, since precipitating factors can be avoided, or lifestyle changes made in order to avoid a crisis.

In acute intermittent porphyria (inherited in an autosomal dominant manner), the central nervous system may be involved and anxiety, depression, disorientation, hallucinations, and paranoia have been described. Surveys of psychiatric patients suggest that the disease is often unrecognised in those patients. Signs may present in childhood, but more often after puberty.

A useful review of these disorders is given by Deswick and others.[29] There has been considerable work on the genetics of these disorders, which is being constantly updated. It is possible to predict an affected child using antenatal tests, in informative families.

Learning difficulties

In the general population, intelligence levels are closely influenced by those of the parents and siblings. Severe learning difficulties (IQ of 50 or less) have a prevalence of about 3/1,000, and the parental IQ is usually normal. In some cases, a clear genetic cause can be defined; this may be chromosomal or the result of a single gene mutation. An increasing number of these can now be accurately diagnosed, but those which are recognised remain the minority.

Many of the difficulties in this area in relation to adoption arise from a) the quality of a family history which is available; b) the difficulty in predicting the future, in terms of behaviour and achievement in children who may have only mild learning problems; and c) the fact that a proportion of children for adoption are the offspring of parents who may be of limited intellectual ability themselves, but where no diagnosis has been made.

Chromosomal

Down's syndrome

Chromosome problems are amongst those most easily recognised. Trisomy 21 (commonly known as Down's syndrome) is the most frequent and well known; the diagnosis is usually made soon after birth. Mental retardation is always present, although to a varying degree. If the child is a mosaic (with a proportion of cells having the normal chromosome complement), then their cognitive ability may be less impaired. Additional problems such as congenital heart disease, leukaemia and Alzheimer's disease may complicate Down's syndrome and reduce life expectancy.

Chromosome translocation

Chromosome translocations which are unbalanced are almost invariably associated with mental retardation and other signs peculiar to the chromosomes involved. The condition may arise anew in the presenting child, but the parents of such a child are at risk of carrying the balanced form and having further affected children. They may also have a child who him/herself is a carrier and who should be given genetic counselling in due course since he/she too is at risk of having a child with the unbalanced form. This is especially important since it is possible to identify these chromosomal problems antenatally, and parents can have the choice of whether or not to continue with the pregnancy. These issues may cause difficulty in the context of adoption when it may be impossible to obtain an accurate family history.

Fragile X syndrome

After Down's syndrome, the most common form of mental retardation and learning difficulty (in males) is the Fragile X syndrome. Approximately 1/1,250 males and 1/2,000 females are affected. About 30 per cent of female carriers show features of the syndrome with mental retardation and characteristic speech and behaviour patterns.

The condition derives its name from the microscopic appearance of the X chromosome which has a 'fragile' looking site on microscopy. Recent work has defined the DNA basis of this fragile site and has enabled diagnosis to be more accurate,[30] and prediction of severity possible. There are several other X linked mental retardation syndromes, some whose genes are very close to that of Fragile X syndrome, but genetic testing for these is not yet well developed.

Classical Fragile X syndrome is characterised by mild to moderate mental handicap, where verbal functioning exceeds performance ability leading to relative strength in tasks involving speech and language, but weakness with number work. The ability to think in three dimensions, and undertake tasks requiring co-ordination of vision and hand movement, is also affected. Early developmental milestones may be achieved at the normal time, but intellectual development is slow. Speech and language acquisition is delayed and has a characteristic pattern with frequent repetitions. 'Cluttering' has been used to describe the speech pattern which can be disorganised with frequent tangential comments. Echolalia and hand flapping have been noted.[31] The verbal/performance discrepancy is seen in females who carry the faulty gene.

One of the most disconcerting aspects of this syndrome are the accompanying behaviour problems. The children are inattentive and may be hyperactive, although this can diminish with age. Autistic features (see above) have been described, the most notable being the speech problems. There is also a general shyness in relating to other people, and an aversion to eye contact. Behaviour modification techniques may provide the basis for intervention in classroom problems.

Sons and daughters of a carrier female are at 50 per cent risk of inheriting the faulty X chromosome from their mother. The genetics of the Fragile X syndrome are complex, since a male may be unaffected but have a premutation in the Fragile X gene, which expands when transmitted by his daughters to his grandchildren, and will cause the syndrome to appear in them. Thus in families where an affected male exists, it is very important that an accurate family history is taken, and investigations offered to at risk relatives. Early diagnosis is desirable in order to introduce special education but expectations must be guarded in severely affected cases. Prenatal diagnosis can be offered to carrier women, but the interpretation of results in female carrier foetuses is especially difficult.

Dyslexia

This disorder of specific reading disability tends to aggregate in families. It is unlikely to be a single condition, and there is much debate on the precise definition of the term. Prevalence estimates are as high as 10 per cent in the UK, and more boys appear to be affected than girls. If a parent and sibling are affected the risks for a child of being affected are higher (greater than 10 per cent) than if the parents are normal and a single child is affected (5-10 per cent).

In an attempt to find a major single gene, attention has focused on chromosome 15[32] but later studies have made it clear that dyslexia is very heterogenous in causation[33] and a multifactorial inheritance model is most appropriate for many cases.[34]

As with so many other disorders that involve learning difficulties, prediction of status is not possible by genetic tests on the basis of current knowledge, and is difficult even where a positive family history exists.

The medical assessment of children with learning disorders, or where there is a family history of mental illness, will continue to be one of the most difficult areas in adoption practice. Accurate descriptions and diagnosis must form the basis of further investigation and management. This will usually involve chromosome studies, if feasible, and possibly metabolic and other investigations. Ultimately, however, successful placement will depend on the willingness, tolerance, and compassion of foster carers and adoptive parents who can see beyond the diagnosis (if established) and accept certain risks for themselves and the child who needs a new family.

References

1 McGuffin et al, *Childhood Disorders*, 174-191, Seminars in Psychological Genetics, Gaskill for Royal College of Psychiatrists, London, 1994.

2 Murrell J, Farlow M, Ghetti B, Benson M, 'A mutation in the amyloid precursor protein associated with hereditary Alzheimer's disease', *Science*, 254:97-9, 1991.

3 Schellenberg G, Bird T, Wijsman E, et al, 'Genetic linkage evidence for a familial Alzheimer's disease locus on chromosome 14', *Science*, 258:668-71, 1992.

4   Van Duijn C M, de Knijff P, Cruts M, et al, 'Apolipoprotein E4 allele in a population-based study of early onset Alzheimer's disease', *Nature Genetics*, 7:74-78, 1994.

5   Munoz-Garcia D, Ludwin S K, 'Classic and generalised variants of Pick's disease: a clinicopathological, ultrastructural and immunocytochemical comparative study', *Annals of Neurology*, 16:467-80, 1984.

6   Collinge J, Palmer M S, Sidle K C L, et al, 'Familial Pick's disease and dementia in frontal lobe dementia of non-Alzheimer type are not variants of prion disease' (Letter), *Journal of Neurology, Neurosurgery and Psychiatry*, 57:762-68, 1994.

7   Huntington's Disease Collaborative Research Group, 'A novel gene containing a trinucleotide repeat which is expanded and unstable on Huntington's disease chromosomes', *Cell*, 72:971-983, 1993.

8   Simpson S A, Besson J, Alexander D, et al, 'One hundred requests for predictive testing for Huntington's disease', *Clinical Genetics*, 41:326-330, 1992.

9   Clarke A, 'The genetic testing of children', *Journal of Medical Genetics*, 31:785-797, 1994.

10 Roberts G W, 'Schizophrenia: the cellular biology of a functional psychosis', *Trends in Neurosciences*, 13:6, 207-211, 1990.

11 O'Callaghan E, Gibson T, Colohan H A, et al, 'Risk of schizophrenia in adults born after obstetric complications and their association with early onset of illness: a controlled study', *British Medical Journal*, 305:1256-1259, 1992.

12 Seeman P, et al, 'Dopamine D4 receptors elevated in schizophrenia', *Nature*, 365:441, 1993.

13 Tsuang M T, 'Genetics, epidemiology and search for causes of schizophrenia', *American Journal of Psychiatry*, 151(1):3-6, 1994, USA.

14 Harper P S, *Practical Genetic Counselling*, Fourth Edition, Butterworth-Heinemann Ltd, 1993.

15 Cadoret R J, 'Evidence for genetic inheritance of primary affective disorder in adoptees', *American Journal of Psychiatry*, 135:463-466, 1978, USA.

16 Berrettini W H, Ferraro T N, Goldin L R, et al, 'Chromosome 18 markers and manic depressive illness: evidence for a susceptibility gene', *Proceedings of the National Academy of Sciences*, 91:5918-21, 1994.

17 Straub R E, Lehner T, Luo Y, et al, 'A possible vulnerability locus for bipolar affective disorder on chromosome 21q22.3', *Nature Genetics*, 8:291-296, 1994.

18 Baron M, Straub R E, Lehner T, et al, 'Bipolar disorder and linkage to Xq28', *Nature Genetics*, 7:461, 1994.

19 Theilgaard A, 'Psychological study of XYY and XXY men', in Ratcliffe S G, Paul N, (eds) *Prospective Studies on Children with Sex Aneuploidy*, March of Dimes Birth Defects Foundation, Birth Defects: Orig Art Series 22(3): 277-292, 1986.

21 Editorial, 'What is to be done with the XYY Fetus?' *British Medical Journal*, 1:1519-1520, 1979.

22 Riccardi V M, *Neurofibromatosis*, 2nd Edition, 1992, The Johns Hopkins University Press. Pauls D L, Raymond C L, Stevenson J M, et al 'A family study of Gilles de la Tourette syndrome', *American Journal of Medical Genetics*, 48:154-63, 1991, USA.

23 Comings De, Comings B G, 'Clinical and genetic relationships between autism-pervasive developmental disorder and Tourette syndrome: a study of 19 cases', *American Journal of Medical Genetics*, 39:180-191, 1991, USA.

24 Van de Wetering B J M, Heutink P, 'The genetics of the Gilles de la Tourette syndrome: a review', *Journal of Laboratory and Clinical Medicine*, 121:638-45, 1993.

25 Gillberg C, 'The neurobiology of infantile autism', *Journal of Child Psychology and Psychiatry*, 29,3:257-266, 1988.

26 Rutter M, *Autism: A reappraisal of concepts and treatment*, Rutter M, and E Schopler, (eds), New York and London, Plenum Press, 1978.

27 McKusick V, *Mendelian Inheritance in Man*, tenth edn, The Johns Hopkins University Press, 1992, USA.

28 Coleman M, Gillberg C, *The Biology of the Autistic Syndromes*, second edn, New York: Praeger, 1987, USA.

29 Desnick R J, Roberts A G, Anderson K E, *The Inherited Porphyrias: Principles and Practice of Medical Genetics*, (eds) Emery A E, and Rimoin D L, Churchill and Livingstone, 1990.

30 Warren St, Nelson D L, 'Advances in molecular analyses of Fragile X syndrome', *Journal of American Medical Association*, 271 (7) 552-3, 1994, USA.

31 Turk J, 'Fragile X syndrome: a common cause of mental retardation', *Maternal and Child Health*, July:228-232, 1991.

32 Smith S D, 'A genetic analysis of specific reading disability', *Genetic Aspects of Speech and Language*, 169-78, Academic Press, 1983, USA.

33 Smith S D, Pennington B F, Kimberling W J, Ing P S, 'Familial dyslexia: use of genetic linkage data to define subtypes', *Journal American Academy of Childhood & Adolescent Psychiatry*, 29, 2:204-13, 1990, USA.

34 Finucci J M, Childs B, 'Dyslexia: Family studies, genetic aspects of speech and language disorders', 157-166, Academic Press, 1983, USA.

9　Cancer genetics

Dr Deepthi de Silva

This chapter aims to discuss the background of cancer genetics with particular reference to the inherited predisposition to cancer. It looks at specific cancer syndromes and their management, and discusses the benefits, or otherwise, of genetic testing, and the consequent need for counselling.

Introduction

Malignant disease is a major cause of mortality and morbidity in Britain, with around one in three people at risk of developing a malignancy in their lifetime. All malignancies are the result of genetic events within cells but these occur by chance and most cancer patients do not pass on a cancer predisposition to their children. However, a proportion of individuals with cancer (around 5–10 per cent) have an inherited predisposition to the development of their disease. These cancer families are characterised by the young age of onset of the affected individuals, the multiplicity of the tumours, and the occurrence of rare tumours within a family. Family members at risk may benefit from screening investigations to identify tumours at a pre-symptomatic or benign stage when the treatment has a better outcome. Individuals with a suspicious family history are seen at cancer family clinics, where they can get information about the significance of the family history, risks to themselves and information regarding the availability of screening and genetic testing. Genetic testing enables more accurate identification of at risk individuals, although at present it is limited to few conditions. The identification of genes involved in the predisposition to common cancers (breast, colon) in the future may allow a larger number of individuals to make an informed choice about genetic testing to predict if they have an inherited cancer predisposition and about screening and preventive therapy. This will usually depend on the availability of accurate information about family medical history, which may not be available to adopted people.

General background

Cancer is a common cause of death and ill health in most parts of the developed world. It is estimated to affect one in three adults at some stage in their lives and deaths from cancer for most ages rank first or second among the leading causes of mortality. The common cancers in women include those of the breast (20 per cent), colon and rectum (12 per cent) lung (9 per cent) and ovary (4 per cent). Among men, lung (26 per cent), colon and rectum (11 per cent), prostate (9 per cent), and stomach (7 per cent), are the commonest tumours.[1] There is a gradually increasing incidence of cancer in the general population, which may partly reflect improved diagnosis and detection. The incidence of cancer increases generally from the age of 40 years.

The exact cause of cancer remains uncertain although a few carcinogens have been implicated in the causation of some malignancies. Of these the commonest is tobacco, which has been implicated in cancers of the lung, other tissues of the respiratory tract, and bladder among others. Exposure to ionising radiation accounts for less than one per cent of cancers (breast, thyroid, marrow, bone). Drugs, including some used to treat cancer, have similarly been suggested as possible carcinogens. The mechanisms of cancer development will be discussed later in the section on genetics.

The treatments for cancers vary widely and encompass surgery, radiotherapy, chemotherapy and immune therapy. Although the prognosis for treated cancers are improving, especially in the childhood leukaemias and lymphomas, there is a high mortality rate associated with the common cancers. As a result, there is an increasing emphasis on cancer prevention. Primary screening (advice on stopping smoking, healthy diets), secondary screening (breast and cervical screening), and tertiary screening (individuals who have already developed a cancer but are at risk of other cancers) are already available and intended to diagnose tumours at a presymptomatic or benign stage. Screening targeted at people with an inherited predisposition has been suggested as a method of reducing the cancer incidence or mortality in some families, and it is this group which is of most concern within adoption.

Scientific background

A tumour is defined as an abnormal mass of tissue, the growth of which exceeds and is unco-ordinated with that of the normal tissues and continues in the same manner after the cessation of the stimuli which have initiated it.[2] All tumours arise as the result of the accumulation of different gene mutations within genes which normally control growth, differentiation and DNA repair. Cancer is therefore invariably a genetic disease at the cellular level. The exact causes of the mutations are not always identifiable but environmental carcinogens such as tobacco and some viruses have been implicated. Most cancers are due to these genetic changes occurring *during life* and are therefore *sporadic*, with no likelihood of an inherited predisposition to other family members.

The genetic alterations occurring in cancers have been studied by looking at the chromosomes (cytogenetics) and changes in the DNA (molecular genetics). The first consistent chromosomal change associated with cancer was identified by Norwell and Hughes who described a rearrangement of two chromosomes, called a translocation, in chronic myeloid leukaemia – known as the Philadelphia chromosome. Since then, other consistent primary chromosome abnormalities have been recognised in tumours.[3] The mechanism of chromosome changes includes loss of part or whole of the chromosome, translocation, or the gain of extra chromosomal material.[4]

A rare group of syndromes inherited as *autosomal recessive* are characterised by an increased number of chromosome breakages being observed under certain laboratory conditions. These include ataxia telangiectasia, Fanconi anaemia and xeroderma pigmentosum.

At the molecular level the genes involved can be separated into two main groups. Genes that have a positive effect on cell growth are the 'proto-oncogenes' which are activated to form *oncogenes*; the genes with a negative effect on cell growth are termed *tumour suppressor* genes.

Over 40 proto-oncogenes and oncogenes have been identified[5,6] and they behave as *dominant* genes at the cell level. Diseases caused by oncogenes are rare but include the dominantly inherited family cancer syndrome 'multiple endocrine neoplasia type 2' (MEN 2),[7] characterised by the occurrence of medullary carcinoma of thyroid and phaechromocytoma.

Tumour suppressor genes exert a negative effect on cell growth and function is lost when *both* copies are inactivated. Hence these genes' actions are *recessive* at the cell level.[8]

Most inherited cancer syndromes are the result of a germline (ie. inherited) mutation of a tumour suppressor gene, with a mutation in the other member of the gene pair occurring during life (Fig. 1). Although recessive at the cell level, cancer syndromes resulting from a germline mutation of a tumour suppressor gene behave as if they are inherited as *autosomal dominants*. They have been identified in a number of cancers and the most common of these are listed in Table 1.

Table 1

Examples of inherited cancer syndromes associated with tumour suppressor genes

1. Familial adenomatous polyposis
2. Familial retinoblastoma
3. Tuberous sclerosis 2
4. Familial breast–ovarian cancer
5. Li-Fraumeni syndrome
6. Neurofibromatosis Type 1
7. Neurofibromatosis Type 2

Figure 1

The two step inactivation of a tumour suppressor gene

Germline Mutation	+	Chance Mutation	→	Familial Retinoblastoma
Chance Mutation	+	Chance Mutation	→	Sporadic Retinoblastoma

In the familial form of retinoblastoma, an inherited mutation of the retinoblastoma (Rb) gene is present in all the retinal cells and the second copy of the gene is inactivated by chance events. In the sporadic cases, both copies of the Rb gene within a retinal cell are inactivated by chance events

Recently another type of gene has been identified which predisposes to cancer when damaged. These are genes involved in the identification and repair of DNA mistakes[9] and have been implicated in familial bowel cancer.

In the development of most cancers, multiple mutations involving both tumour suppressor genes and oncogenes occur in a single cell. This accumulation of mutations occurs in all cancers irrespective of whether they are familial (with an inherited gene mutation) or sporadic (chance mutations during life). Each new mutation confers a growth advantage to the cell, leading to the formation of a group of daughter cells with the new mutation (clonal expansion). The sequence of steps in the development of a colon cancer is a useful model to demonstrate the multistep progression of cancer (see Figure 2 below, modified from Vogelstein et al).[10]

Figure 2 **The multi-step progression of colon cancer**

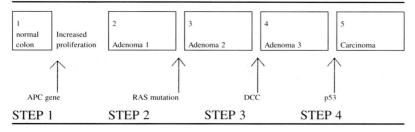

Specific cancer syndromes and their management
1. Familial breast and ovarian cancer
Inherited predisposition is the major predisposing factor for up to 10 per cent of all cases of breast cancer. Three genes have been identified in some of the families with an inherited predisposition, but other genes may also be involved.

Mutations of the p53 gene are common in many sporadic cancers when they arise as one of the sequence of genetic events within a tumour but in the Li-Fraumeni syndrome, a p53 mutation is inherited from the sperm or egg cell and, as a result, all the individuals cells have a faulty copy of this gene.[11] Carriers of this mutation are at risk of numerous childhood malignancies including soft tissue and bone sarcomas, brain and adrenal tumours, melanoma and breast cancer in young women. The p53 gene has been characterised and direct mutation detection is possible, enabling the identification of the individuals at risk. Such families are likely to account for less than one per cent of all the familial breast cancers. In spite of its rarity, it is important to identify these families as the first degree relatives of affected individuals are at 50 per cent risk of cancer occurring in childhood or in young adults.

The second gene implicated in the inherited predisposition to early onset breast cancer is the recently isolated BRCA1 gene on chromosome 17q21.[12,13] It is likely to be important in the genetic predisposition to breast cancer in most families with breast and epithelial ovarian cancer, and a proportion of families with early onset breast cancer. Identification of family members who are gene carriers can be performed by a DNA linkage study if the family structure is suitable. Once the mutation within the BRCA1 gene is identified in an affected individual, other family members can be offered genetic predictive testing. Carriers of the mutation have about an 80 per cent lifetime risk[14] (compared with the population risk of around 8 per cent) of developing a malignancy related to this gene. A third gene called BRCA2 has now been localised to chromosome 13q in some families with male and female breast cancer.[15] Women with a family history of breast cancer not typical of the BRCA2 or Li-Fraumeni can be offered risk assessments based on epidemiological data.[16]

Mammography is the method of breast screening that is used most widely but it has disadvantages in being difficult to interpret in women under 50 (those most at risk of familial cancer) and involving exposure to radiation. Screening for ovarian cancer using ultrasound can be difficult. Some women opt for prophylactic surgery to reduce their risk. The value of medical therapy in breast cancer prevention is being evaluated.[17]

2. Familial adenomatous polyposis (FAP)

This is a rare colon cancer predisposing syndrome caused by a single gene (APC) defect and accounting for less than one per cent of colon cancers. FAP is characterised by the presence of over 100 growths, called adenomatous polyps, within the colon and rectum, which develop from the teenage years. Untreated, the polyps invariably progress to malignancy. Treatment at present involves resecting the colon and rectum. Affected individuals are also at risk of other tumours and require careful follow up. Retinal pigmentary changes called CHRPEs (congenital hypertrophy of the retinal pigment epithelium) are present from birth in some FAP patients and can be a useful indicator of gene carriers.

FAP is an autosomal dominant condition but around one third of new cases represent new mutations. There are well established management protocols for the identification and treatment of affected and at risk individuals[18,19] and the establishment of genetic registers has enabled this to occur more efficiently. Direct gene mutation analysis is available and can detect the fault in approximately two-thirds of cases.

3. Hereditary non polyposis colon cancer (HNPCC)

This may account for up to 10 per cent of all colon cancers.[20] The criteria for the clinical diagnosis of HNPCC are strict (three or more family members affected, with two of these being first degree relatives, one member under the age of 50 years and two or more generations of a family affected)[21] but more families may now be identified following the characterisation of two genes implicated in some HNPCC families. HNPCC is subdivided into type 1 and 2 depending on the presence, respectively, of colon cancer only or colon and other cancer within the families.[22] The other sites of cancer include the endometrium, larynx, stomach, renal tract, pancreas and ovary. The age of onset of the tumours vary from the early 20s onwards.

The purpose of identification of the families is to offer screening using colonoscopy (examination of the bowel by a flexible fibreoptic telescope), which enables the identification of premalignant, adenomatous polyps prior to their progression to carcinomas. Screening for the other tumours occurring in the family is also recommended. Genetic diagnosis is at an early stage.[23,24] This includes family linkage studies, detection of DNA instability in the carcinomas compared with the patient's normal tissue and gene mutation detection in appropriate cases.

4. Neurofibromatosis

(1) Type 1 (von Recklinghausen's disease): This is an autosomal

dominant condition characterised by the presence of skin lumps called neurofibromata, developing from adolescence onwards, plus multiple, rounded brown markings of the skin termed cafe au lait spots, axillary and inguinal freckling, Lisch nodules in the iris of the eye, and bony changes.[25] Affected individuals are at risk of a whole range of other malignancies, particularly central nervous system tumours. The gene involved has been characterised but mutation detection is not routinely available.

(2) Type 2: This is an autosomal dominant condition associated with bilateral acoustic neuromas (tumours of the acoustic nerve within the skull causing deafness and associated with other features) but with a predisposition to other brain tumours (including meningioma, astrocytoma and ependymoma).[26] Skin neurofibromata can occur but the other features of NF1 are not present. The tumour supressor gene implicated has been characterised and is located on chromosome 22.

5. Von Hippel Lindau (VHL) disease

This is an autosomal dominant disorder associated with the risk of developing brain, eye and kidney tumours. (The associated tumours include cerebellar, brain stem and spinal haemangiblastomas, retinal angiomas, renal carcinomas among others.) The clinical diagnostic criteria and protocols for the managenment of VHL families are available.[27] Linkage or mutation analysis can be used to identify gene carriers.

Psychosocial aspects and counselling of families with a cancer predisposition

Counselling offered to families with a cancer predisposition involves the following steps. A full family history is required with adequate details of the family members who have been diagnosed as having cancer. These details should be verified by obtaining the hospital records or through cancer registers. Death certificate verification can be performed although the histology details are not easily traceable with this method. Pathology details (available through hospital records or cancer registers) are especially useful if linkage studies are planned as tissue sections from deceased individuals can be used to extract DNA.

Verification of reported family histories is essential as some families attribute any debilitating disease to cancer and the reported sites of the tumours can often be inaccurate. Other advantages include information about multiple tumours if they occur, and possible carcinogen exposure.

In the case of an adopted individual, as with anyone else, information required to support a diagnosis of a cancer family syndrome includes the age of onset, site (including multiple tumours), number of affected individuals in the family and their relationship to each other. If a suspicious family history is obtained, the affected family member's full name, date of birth, address, hospital where treatment was offered, and year of death, will be required to verify the history at a later stage.

Counselling involves discussion of the family history and its possible significance to the proband. Risk assessments are offered based on the research data from population studies or, in the families with a clearly inherited predisposition, based on the pattern of inheritance. Information also discussed, if appropriate, includes the availability and benefits of screening tests, genetic testing and prophylactic therapy. The ideal place for such counselling is probably a combined screening clinic or a genetic clinic.

If genetic predictive testing is planned, further counselling is usual to enable the individuals to make an informed decision about the benefits and disadvantages of such tests. As with other predictive tests, the psychological effects for the people found to be at either high or low risk may be considerable but has not been fully evaluated. There are implications for employment and insurance which have not yet been fully assessed. The benefits include more accurate information to base decisions on screening and prophylactic therapy.

At present, only a small number of families can be offered such genetic tests, but as the genetic predisposition to the common cancers (breast and colon in particular) is better defined, more individuals and families are likely to become eligible for such tests.

There is increasing awareness in the general population of the significance of a family history of cancer and many cancer clinics have experience of reassuring those individuals whose family history is not suspicious of an inherited risk of cancer (eg. the affected relative's age, affected relative being only distantly related). Uncertainty or misinformation about a cancer family history may be a cause of anxiety, especially in adopted individuals, and lack of information may be a barrier to reassurance.

Some of the inherited cancer syndromes can predispose to medical problems or learning difficulties. These include tuberous sclerosis, neurofibromatosis and the rare chromosomal fragility syndromes. Knowledge of the family history may enable the clinicians to diagnose the condition earlier and also avoid unnecessary or potentially harmful investigations. The identification and follow up of a cancer family history predisposing to childhood cancer will be of benefit for the adopted child, as appropriate screening or preventive therapy can be initiated. In the diseases where the onset is in the second or third decade (eg. familial adenomatous polyposis) children who have been informed of the risks and have understood the screening regimes are more willing to comply than those who have been informed later in life.

In the cancer syndromes with an adult onset of tumours, the information is not immediately of benefit to the adopted individual and it may be preferable to inform the adult at their request. Once an adult adopted person has requested the information, it would be ideal if the genetic unit undertaking the counselling have access to the required information to expedite their work.

The genetic testing of individuals at risk of cancer can pose many ethical problems. As with non-adopted individuals, these include the psychological effects of a positive or negative test result, the management of high risk individuals, the insurance and employment implications and the technical problems of offering such tests.

The genetic testing of children can only be justified if there is a risk of a childhood onset disease, when screening or preventive therapy can be started, or if a child has developed symptoms, to confirm the diagnosis.

In the case of adopted people, the availability of genetic testing will pose even greater problems. Linkage studies will be difficult or impossible, as the informed consent of the birth family may not always be available. Similarly, DNA specimens from the key family members will be difficult to obtain. Specific mutation detection can be offered in a few genetic conditions with a predisposition to cancer (eg. MEN2, Li-Fraumeni) but this might be impossible without the information about the causative mutation in the affected family member.

The rights of the individual likely to benefit from genetic testing (the right to knowledge in order to make an informed choice about screening or preventive therapy) is likely to be the important issue with adopted people, but great caution has to be exercised both about the technical limitations and ethical issues raised by such tests.

Genetic predisposition to cancer is an important recent development in medicine and one which is likely to have a significant social impact. As awareness in the general population increases, a growing number of individuals are requesting counselling and screening. An accurate family history of cancer is vital in the assessment of inherited cancer risks and adopted individuals are at present likely to be at a distinct disadvantage compared with others in benefiting from the developments occurring in genetic screening and preventive therapy.

References

1 *Cancer statistics: registrations, England and Wales 1983*, HMSO, 1986.

2 *Muir's Textbook of Pathology*, ed. Anderson J R, 10th edn. Edward Arnold, 1976.

3 Mitelman F, *Catalog of chromosome aberrations in cancer*, Alan R. Liss Inc, 1988, USA.

4 Heim S, and Mitelman F, 'Non random chromosome abnormalities in cancer: an overview', *Cancer Cytogenetics*, pp 23-37. Alan R. Liss Inc, 1987, USA.

5 Hodgson S V, and Maher E R, *A practical guide to human cancer genetics*, Cambridge University Press, 1993.

6 Bishop J M, 'Molecular themes in oncogenesis', *Cell*, 64:234-48, 1991.

7 Mulligan L M, Kwok J B, Healey C S, et al, 'Germline mutations of the RET oncogene in multiple endocrine neoplasia type 2A', *Nature*, 363:458-460, 1993.

8 Knudson A G, 'Mutation and cancer: Statistical study of retinoblastoma', *Proc Natu Acad Sci*, 68:820-3, 1971.

9 Wooster R, Cleton-Jansen, A M, Collins N, et al, 'Instability of short tandem

repeats (microsatellites) in human cancers', *Nature Genetics* 6:152-156, 1994.

10 Fearon E and Vogelstein B, 'A genetic model for colorectal tumourigenesis', *Cell*, 61:759-767, 1990.

11 Malkin D, Li F P, Strong L C, et al, 'Germline mutations in a familial syndrome of breast cancer, sarcomas and other neoplasms', *Science*, 250:1233-1238, 1990.

12 Hall J M, Lee M K, Newman et al, 'Linkage of early onset familial breast cancer to chromosome 17q21', *Science*, 250:1684-1689, 1990.

13 Miki Y, Swenson J, Shattuck-Eidens D, et al, 'A strong candidate for the breast and ovarian cancer susceptibility gene BRCA1', *Science*, 206:66-71, 1994.

14 Ford D, Easton D, Bishop T, et al, 'Risks of cancer in BRCA1 mutation carriers', *Lancet*, 343:692-695, 1994.

15 Wooster R, Neuhausen S, Mangion J, et al, 'Localisation of a breast cancer susceptibility gene BRCA2, to chromosome 13q 12-13', *Science*, 265:2088-2090, 1994.

16 Houlston R S, McCarter E, Parbhoo S, et al, 'Family history and risk of breast cancer', *Journal of Medical Genetics*, 29:154-157, 1992.

17 Powles T, 'The case for clinical trials of tamoxifen for prevention of breast cancer', *Lancet*, 340:1145-1147, 1992.

18 Giardiello F M, Offerhaus G J, Traboulsi E I, et al, 'The value of combined phenotypic markers in identifying inheritance of familial adenomatous polyposis', *Gut*, 32:1170-1174, 1991.

19 Rhodes M, Bradburn D M, 'Overview of screening and management of familial adenomatous polyposis', *Gut*, 33:125-131, 1992.

20 Mecklin J P, 'Frequency of hereditary nonpolyposis colorectal carcinoma', *Gastroenterology*, 93:1021-1025, 1986.

21 Vasen H F, Mecklin J P, Khan P M, Lynch H T, 'Hereditary non-polyposis colorectal cancer', *Lancet*, 338:877, 1991.

22 Mecklin J P, Jarvinen H J, 'Clinical features of colorectal cancer in the cancer family syndrome', *Dis. colon rectum*, 29:160-164, 1986.

23 Leach F S, Nicolaides C S, Papadopoulos N, et al, 'Mutations of the mutS

homolog in hereditary nonpolyposis colorectal cancer', *Cell*, 75:1215-1225, 1993.

24 Lindblom A, Tannergard P, Werelius B, Nordenskjold M, 'Genetic mapping of a second locus predisposing to hereditary nonpolyposis colon cancer', *Nature genetics*, 5:279-282, 1993.

25 Huson S M, Compston D A S, Harper P S, 'A genetic study of Von Recklinghausen's neurofibromatosis in South Wales. 2. Guidelines for genetic counselling', *Journal of Medical Genetics*, 26:712-21, 1989.

26 Evans D G R, Huson S, Neary W, et al, 'A genetic study of type 2 neurofibromatosis in the north west of England and the UK: prevalence, mutation rate, fitness and confirmation of maternal transmission effect on severity', *Journal of Medical Genetics*, 29 (12):841-846, 1992.

27 Maher E R, Yates J RW, Harries R, et al, 'Clinical features and natural history of Von Hippel-Lindau disease', *Quarterly Journal of Medicine*, 77:1151-63, 1990.

10 Congenital heart disease, adult cardiovascular disease and diabetes

Dr John C S Dean

Congenital heart disease is one of the most common types of birth defect or malformation encountered by paediatricians, whilst adult cardiovascular disorders are among the most common health problems in industrialised countries. As the genetic basis of many individual conditions is increasingly understood the possibility of accurate predictive testing may be a reality in the foreseeable future. Predictive testing may open up new opportunities for medical and lifestyle interventions to improve long-term health but, as with most hereditary disorders, awareness of risk will depend on a knowledge of family medical history. Adopted people may therefore be significantly disadvantaged as these developments take place. This chapter outlines recent advances in our understanding in some detail and provides the interested reader, especially the medical adviser, with a broad ranging overview of a complex, and sometimes confusing, topic.

Congenital heart disease is usually defined as cardiac malformation, present at birth, and is a common problem in the newborn period (6 per 1,000 live births).[1] Around 10 per cent of congenital heart disease is caused by chromosomal anomalies such as Down's syndrome or Turner syndrome, and the majority of other cases are multifactorial. Most such chromosome disorders are 'sporadic', and therefore have a low recurrence risk both for siblings and offspring of an affected person, and similarly the recurrence risk for multifactorial disease is usually low. However, in amongst the multifactorial cases are a number of single gene disorders and inherited chromosome microdeletions, where the recurrence risks may be substantial, and it is here that recent developments are beginning to shed light on the aetiology of cardiac malformations.

Isolated congenital heart disease

In assessing the recurrence risk for the siblings or future offspring of an infant or child with congenital heart disease, there are two main aspects to consider. Firstly, is there a family history of congenital heart disease, or other congenital malformation which might suggest a Mendelian (ie. single gene) pattern of inheritance, and secondly, does the child in question have any other clinical features that might lead to a syndrome diagnosis? A syndrome is simply the term given to a recognisable pattern of anomalies or malformations which occur together in a consistent pattern, eg. Down's syndrome (due to an extra chromosome 21). A child or adult with isolated congenital heart disease is unlikely to have an abnormal chromosome number. The majority of such cases will be multifactorial and there is a substantial amount of empirical data available to help in assessing the risk, based on the anatomical lesion present. There are differences in estimated risks in different studies, and the risks for offspring of affected parents are of necessity based on small numbers, but the area has been comprehensively reviewed by Nora et al;[1] Table 1 is adapted from his data. Contained within these studies are families in which the pattern of recurrence would suggest a Mendelian gene, for example, hypoplastic left heart has been recorded to be inherited apparently as an autosomal recessive trait,[2] patent ductus arteriosus as an autosomal dominant,[3] and supravalvular aortic stenosis as an autosomal dominant.[4,5,6] Within the group with conotruncal abnormalities (interrupted aortic arch, coarctation of the aorta, outflow tract anomalies), are patients with CATCH 22,[7] of which more later. In addition, recurrences are not always of the same cardiac lesion (at most, only 60 per cent of affected siblings of patients with a VSD (Vertricular Septal Defect) also have a VSD),[8] and this information should be borne in mind when counselling. Unravelling the embryological and genetic mechanisms underlying these observations is one of the great challenges facing medicine today, and at last some are beginning to fall to the investigations of the molecular embryologists.

Syndromes with congenital heart disease

Although cardiac defects are often present in isolation, they may also form part of a syndrome, and it is always important to seek other malformations in any child in which one has been identified. Cardiac malformation is part of many syndromes, but I will discuss only some of the more common ones, or those which illustrate recent advances.

Table 1

Probable recurrence risk (shown in percentages)

Defect	1 affected sib %	2 affected sibs %	Father affected %	Mother affected %
Ventricular septal defect	3	10	2.5	9.5
Atrial septal defect	2.5	8	1.5	6
Patent ductus arteriosus	3	10	2	4
Fallot's tetralogy	2.5	8	1.5	2.5
Arteriovenous canal defect	2.5	10	1	14
Pulmonary stenosis	2	6	2	6.5
Aortic stenosis	2	6	5	18
Coarctation of aorta	2	6	2.5	4
Hypoplastic left heart	3	10		
Pulmonary atresia	1			
Common truncus	1			
Tricuspid atresia	1			
Ebstein's anomaly	1			

Noonan Syndrome

This disorder is quite well known to many paediatricians and consists of pulmonary stenosis (narrowing of the pulmonary artery and/or valve) as the most common heart problem, short stature, neck webbing, cubitus valgus, and some typical facial features including ptosis, down slanting eyes, and low set ears. Noonan syndrome is a dominantly inherited disorder although about half of all newly diagnosed cases are new events in a family.

Features resembling Noonan are often found in Neurofibromatosis type 1 (NF1 or Von Recklinghausen's disease). Because the NF1 gene is very large and appears to contain other genes within it, it was initially thought that the Noonan gene might be one of these internal genes. However, the autosomal dominant Noonan families do not show genetic linkage to the NF1 gene on chromosome 17, but are mostly linked to a gene on chromosome 12.[9] It is possible that what we call Noonan Syndrome is a pattern of developmental anomalies that may have many causes.

The Noonan-like syndromes (Cardio-Facio-Cutaneous syndrome and Costello syndrome)

A number of children have been described who have Noonan features, some of which are of atypical severity, and additional anomalies. In Cardio-Facio-Cutaneous syndrome,[10] the cardiac malformation is more commonly ASD than pulmonary stenosis, and ectodermal (hypotrichosis and follicular hyperkeratosis) and neuro developmental features are more prominent than in Noonan syndrome. Cardio-Facio-Cutaneous syndrome itself overlaps with Costello syndrome[11] which is characterised by similar Noonan-like features with ectodermal manifestations, but also includes skin laxity and hyperpigmentation. Costello also includes increased rather than low/normal birth weight, a tendency to cardiomyopathy as the cardiac lesion, and the occurrence of peri-oral verrucoid lesions in later childhood. There may well be other Noonan-like syndromes awaiting delineation, but whether these are truly separate genetic conditions, variants on a spectrum, or simply a common developmental response to a variety of injurious stimuli is unknown – we await the discovery of the molecular mechanisms to clarify this issue.

Limb defect syndromes

Another embryological association is that of cardiac malformation with limb defects. The best known syndromes in this context are the Holt-Oram, Roberts and Fanconi syndromes. In Holt-Oram syndrome, inherited as an autosomal dominant, Atrial Septal Defect is found with radial limb anomalies (ranging from digitalisation of the thumb to duplication of the thumb to radial aplasia).[12] Roberts and Fanconi syndromes, like many others, are rather non-specific in their cardiac malformations. Roberts syndrome (autosomal recessive) comprises severe limb reduction defects, facial clefting and cardiac malformations, associated with centromeric puffing on chromosome analysis, and in the autosomal recessive Fanconi syndrome, radial limb reduction defects occur with pancytopenia and non-specific cardiac malformations. Different genes are likely to underlie these syndromes.

CATCH 22 (including DiGeorge syndrome, velocardiofacial syndrome and conotruncal anomaly face syndrome)

The acronym CATCH22 (Cardiac, Abnormal facies, Thymic hypoplasia, Cleft palate, Hypocalcemia) has been suggested recently to cover a group of disorders, initially thought to have different aetiologies, which now appear all to be associated with microdeletion of chromosome 22, band q11.[13] The story begins with the description of DiGeorge syndrome in 1965,[14] comprising thymic hypoplasia, hypoparathyroidism (causing hypocalcemia) and conotruncal cardiac malformation. The embryological connection between these abnormalities (3rd and 4th branchial arch derivatives) was noted and other features such as a characteristic face and cleft palate were described. An association with chromosome 22 (amongst others) dates back to 1981, but it was not until the development of FISH (fluorescent in situ hybridisation) permitted the detection of submicro-scopic deletions of chromosome 22q11 that the extent of the association was understood.[15] DiGeorge is often apparently sporadic, and this is probably because the deletion is often sporadic. The deletion can be familial, however, and it soon became clear that this was the cause of the phenotypically similar, but hereditary (autosomal dominant) disorder Velocardiofacial (or Shprintzen) syndrome.[16] Peculiar facies (bulbous nose, malformed ears), cleft palate/palatal insufficiency and conotruncal cardiac malformation characterise this disorder. Patients with related conditions (eg. conotruncal anomaly face syndrome), and some with isolated cardiac malformations, familial[17] and otherwise, have also been found to have deletions, so the true spectrum of CATCH22 is more variable than was first suspected. Having made the diagnosis in one child, it is unwise to pronounce on whether the disorder is familial or not, without at least investigating parental blood samples (by FISH). Once the deletion has arisen, it may be transmitted to offspring, and behaves as a variable autosomal dominant Mendelian trait. Recently, a gene (Tuple

1) has been isolated from the deleted region.[18] Its function is probably as a regulator of other genes, and it may be the major contributor to the CATCH22 phenotype.

Williams syndrome

Although rare and usually sporadic, I include this disorder as it too has proved to be a chromosomal microdeletion syndrome, this time involving the elastin locus on chromosome 7.[19] Williams syndrome comprises supravalvular aortic stenosis, hypercalcemia and characteristic facies. Patients may later develop a superficial congeniality, which masks their degree of learning disability, and which has become known as a 'cocktail party manner'. Mutations in the elastin gene cause familial supravalvular-aortic stenosis, and it is possible that Williams syndrome is a contiguous gene syndrome, ie. that it results from disruption by deletion of the elastin gene and one or more neighbouring genes. The deletion is, however, usually too small to be detected other than by FISH.

CHARGE association

There are a number of other disorders where congenital heart disease is a major component, of which perhaps the best known is the CHARGE[20] association (Coloboma, Heart disease, choanal Atresia, Retardation of postnatal growth and development, Genital hypoplasia and Ear anomalies). This is an association rather than a syndrome because the underlying aetiology remains unknown, although 22q11 deletion has been seen in a few cases. It usually has a low recurrence risk.

Environmental factors

It is important not to forget the environmental risk factors for congenital heart disease. Foetal Alcohol Syndrome is associated with cardiac malformation, usually VSD, Fallot's tetralogy, or ASD. It can be recognised by the typical facies (smooth philtrum, thin upper lip), relative microcephaly and developmental delay, tremulousness and hyperactivity, with a history of chronic maternal alcohol ingestion of greater than seven units per week. Maternal drug therapy, for example, with anticonvulsants or lithium may cause foetal cardiac malformation. Lithium has been associated with Ebstein's anomaly of the heart. The risk of discontinuing the treatment often outweighs the risk of malformation, however. Maternal illnesses such as rubella, diabetes, systemic lupus erythematosus and phenylketonuria are all associated with increased risk of congenital heart disease.[21] These all illustrate the 'embryological insult' aspect of cardiac malformation.

Adult cardiovascular disease

Adult onset single gene disorders

These disorders are in some ways more difficult to deal with in an adoption situation than the congenital malformation syndromes, as there may be no conclusive clinical evidence that a child is affected until the approach of adulthood. In addition, many adults with hereditary heart disorders are not aware of the hereditary nature of their condition, or choose to ignore it, and so family history information to confirm a suspected diagnosis may be difficult to obtain. The most frequent problems arise with the disorders which predispose to arterial rupture, which include Marfan's syndrome, Ehlers Danlos syndrome type IV, and polycystic kidney disease; these are described below. The cardiomyopathies are another group where diagnostic, treatment and social issues complicate the situation.

Marfan's syndrome

This disorder is well known from medical text books as one of the commonest conditions causing tall stature. It is now acknowledged that it has been over diagnosed in tall people.

It is a variable autosomal dominant disorder of connective tissue, whose principal features are skeletal (tall stature, arachnodactyly, scoliosis, pectus deformities), ocular (lens dislocation, myopia) and cardiovascular (aortic dilatation, dissection and rupture, aortic and mitral valve incompetence).[22] Other features such as thin scars, lumbar striae and dural ectasia may occur. A reduced lifespan occurs because the connective tissue weakness allows the development of aneurysms, particularly of the ascending aorta, which commonly rupture in the third or fourth decades. The risk of rupture correlates with the aortic diameter, usually measured by echocardiography at annual review, and prophylactic aortic surgery[23] is recommended when the diameter exceeds 55mm. The rate of progression of the aortic dilatation is reduced by beta-blocking drugs.[24] The disease was originally mapped to chromosome 15 by family studies in 1990,[25] and abnormalities in the Fibrillin gene (FBN1) have subsequently been demonstrated.[26] In 1994, a second gene causing Marfan's syndrome was found in one family to be on chromosome 3 [27] but so far little is known about this gene. If clinical assessment is inconclusive, presymptomatic diagnosis by gene tracking or family DNA analysis may be possible where there is a large accessible family with a clear history; in small families it may not be possible to determine which gene is the cause. In addition, a proportion of cases are sporadic (new mutations). It is hoped that advances in biochemical assessment of fibrillin handling at a cellular level, and direct mutation analysis may aid diagnosis in the near future. Because the disease is life threatening, and amenable to preventative treatment (beta blockers and prophylactic surgery) are much safer than emergency surgery for a ruptured aortic aneurysm, the importance of the diagnosis cannot be overstressed.

Ehlers Danlos syndrome type IV
The Ehlers Danlos group of syndromes (EDS) are well known for causing excessive elasticity of the skin and joint laxity which often means that people are referred to as being 'double-jointed'. Type IV should not be confused with the milder types where skin and joint laxity with easy bruising are prominent. In EDS IV, skin and joint laxity are often absent, but there is a high incidence of arterial aneurysms (often of cerebral arteries) which may rupture,[28] and of spontaneous bowel perforation in young adults. There is also a characteristic face comprising a thin, pinched nose, with thin skin. The condition is autosomal dominant, and caused by mutations in the type III collagen gene which maps to chromosome 2 band q31. DNA testing and collagen assay in cultured fibroblasts may aid diagnosis. Unfortunately, there is no treatment known to improve prognosis, although awareness of the diagnosis may lead to more rapid and appropriate management of the complications. In this disorder, aneurysm ruptures in unusual sites in otherwise healthy young adults may lead to potentially fatal diagnostic confusion. The burden of knowledge for the patient must not be forgotten, particularly if testing is proposed for a child who cannot give valid consent.

Adult polycystic kidney disease

This is an important condition which does not usually declare itself until adult life and is dominantly inherited (in contrast to infantile polycystic kidney disease which is recessively inherited). Although renal disease is the main aspect of this condition, it is associated with arterial hypertension and berry aneurysms of the cerebral circulation. There are at least two genetic forms[29] which are clinically indistinguishable. However, Type 2 (due to a chromosome 4 gene) is statistically less severe than Type 1 (caused by a chromosome 16 gene). The renal cysts are rarely present at birth, but become detectable by ultrasound scanning through childhood and early adult life. Polycystic kidney disease cannot be reliably excluded by ultrasound until around the age of 30 years.[30] Presymptomatic testing using linked DNA markers is possible but not straightforward because of the genetic heterogeneity. The chromosome 16 gene has recently been identified, which may allow direct mutation testing in the near future.[31] Presymptomatic diagnosis is valuable, as early treatment of complications such as hypertension may improve prognosis.

The cardiomyopathies

Pathological cardiomyopathy may result from many different causes including various infectious agents and acquired metabolic disturbances. The form commonly known as 'hypertrophic cardiomyopathy' is inherited as an autosomal dominant condition in over 50 per cent of cases.[32] In a proportion of the familial cases, the disorder is due to mutation in the ß-myosin heavy chain gene on chromosome 14.[33,34] Like polycystic kidney disease, the diagnosis can be made by ultrasound (echocardiography) but the variability in severity of the disorder means that a normal scan in an individual with a family history is not diagnostic of genetic status. The ECG faces similar limitations. Presymptomatic DNA testing is possible, if the family is known to be chromosome 14 linked, and mutation testing may be useful in some instances. Again this is a disorder where early treatment of an asymptomatic individual is of uncertain benefit, and DNA testing should therefore only be carried out where there is fully informed consent of the tested individual. In the case of an adopted person, details of the family history risk, if known, should be given to the individual when he or she reaches maturity, with appropriate medical and counselling backup.

Dilated cardiomyopathy may also be familial, and autosomal dominant[35] and X-linked recessive types have been described. The X-linked type is due to unusual mutations in the dystrophin gene[36] (dystrophin is the gene usually associated with Duchenne and Becker muscular dystrophies). In one family,[37] mitochondrial DNA deletions were seen in cardiac muscle, but it was not possible to say whether the disease was due to an autosomal or mitochondrial gene. A genetic polymorphism at the angiotensin-converting enzyme gene may contribute to severity.[38]

The occurrence of congenital heart block in the offspring of mothers with systemic lupus erythematosus is well known,[39] and there are other (usually sporadic) causes of complete heart block. Supraventricular tachycardia may result from other forms of aberrant conduction such as the Wolf-Parkinson-White syndrome. This is usually said to be sporadic, but autosomal dominant families have been described.[40] Given that many individuals with accessory conduction pathways may be asymptomatic and therefore not have had ECGs, it is possible that Wolf-Parkinson-White and the related Lown-Ganong-Levine syndrome may be familial more often than is suspected.

The Long QT syndromes

Perhaps the most important familial causes of arrhythmias are the long QT syndromes.[41] The name derives from the increased duration of the QT interval seen on the resting ECG. In the autosomal dominant type, Romano-Ward syndrome, polymorphic ventricular tachycardia is commonly precipitated by sudden emotion (fright) or exertion. The tachycardia is usually self-limiting and results in syncope, pre-syncope or a pseudo-seizure, but it may cause sudden death. Many patients have been misdiagnosed initially as having epilepsy, until an ECG demonstrated the true aetiology of their blackouts. Attacks may be prevented by beta-blockers, sometimes supplemented by permanent pacing, as resting bradycardia can also be a problem in this disorder. It appears that several genes can cause clinically similar types of hereditary long QT syndrome.[42] Genetic testing is therefore very difficult, unless there is an extensive family history. Premature death of family members from arrhythmia can limit the scope of genetic investigations in this disorder. There is also a recessive form of long QT syndrome, known as Jervell-Lange-Neilsen syndrome. The cardiac features are the same as for Romano-Ward, but homozygous affected individuals also suffer from profound congenital sensorineural deafness. This condition is not due to the chromosome 11 gene. It is interesting that heterozygote carriers of this recessive form of long QT syndrome (who are not deaf) may have a prolonged QT interval on their own ECGs, yet rarely suffer arrhythmia, in contrast to Romano-Ward patients.

Multifactorial adult cardiovascular diseases

Hypertension

This is a major cause of cardiovascular morbidity in adult life, but is only rarely due to the primary effects of a single gene. It is usually a continuous trait, like height. There is a close correlation in blood pressure between family members, but there are also correlations between spouses, indicating the important role of shared environment in this disorder.[43,44] There are perhaps two important single gene causes of hypertension – polycystic kidney disease which has been discussed earlier, and glucocorticoid responsive hyperaldosteronism.[45] The latter is an autosomal dominant disorder, due to mutation in the gene coding for an enzyme which catalyses both cortisol and aldosterone production. As the name suggests, the condition responds to corticosteroid therapy. It is likely that other genetic causes of hypertension will become apparent over the next few years, but it is likely that the majority of cases will remain multifactorial.

Hyperlipidemias

This is a complex area, in which many genetic factors interact with environmental influences to result in atherosclerotic arterial disease in middle to late adult life.[46,47] In terms of genes, there are those which have a major effect on blood cholesterol and behave as autosomal dominant traits (eg. the LDL receptor gene, the Apolipoprotein B gene) and those which have a modifying influence on the blood lipids. Mutations in the LDL receptor or in the Apolipoprotein B gene cause familial hypercholesterolaemia (FH), where a high serum cholesterol is associated with premature arterial disease in the 30-50 age group (myocardial infarction, stroke, claudication) and, often, subcutaneous and tendinous cholesterol deposits – xanthomas. FH is fairly common (about 1 in 1,000 people have it) but only accounts for a small proportion of premature vascular disease (10-20 per cent).

An important issue is that although the disease is genetic, it is not untreatable – careful control of blood cholesterol from early childhood by diet and, if necessary, drugs, will substantially reduce the risk of premature vascular disease. It is therefore important to ensure that a child at risk of inheriting the disorder is appropriately followed up.

Genetic testing by linked DNA markers is possible for younger individuals whose blood lipids may be non-diagnostic. Because there are many affected heterozygotes in the population, children are born from time to time who are homozygous for an LDL receptor mutation. These children have much more severe hypercholesterolaemia, and frequently develop ischaemic heart disease in their teens or early twenties. They require very close medical supervision to maximise their health and life-expectancy.

Diabetes mellitus
Diabetes is a common disorder within which are a number of clinically, pathologically and genetically separate diseases.

Insulin dependent diabetes mellitus (IDDM)
IDDM[48,49] affects around 0.3 per cent of the population by age 20 in the UK. It does not have a very high concordance rate in monozygotic twins (30 per cent), suggesting that while genetic factors are important, they are not the whole story. Empirically, the lifetime risk of IDDM to the brother or sister of a patient is 6.6 per cent, for the child of a patient 4.9 per cent, and for the parent of an affected child, 2.9 per cent. Around 60 per cent of the inherited component relates to the immune response genes of the HLA class 2 region of chromosome 6. Ninety five per cent of patients have HLA type DR3 or DR4, and DR3/DR4 heterozygotes are at greatest risk (14.3 relative risk).

Specific variants of the DQ gene are also associated with high risk of IDDM. The environmental 'trigger' of IDDM has not yet been identified.

Non-insulin dependent diabetes mellitus (NIDDM)

NIDDM[50,51] is usually a disease of older people, but has a much higher concordance rate in identical twins (90 per cent). Brothers and sisters of an affected patient have a 40 per cent lifetime risk of developing NIDDM, but despite this, the disease does not often follow an obvious Mendelian or single gene pattern of inheritance in families. However, in a subgroup of NIDDM, the so-called maturity onset diabetes of the young (MODY), mutation in the promoter region of the glucokinase gene has been described in a proportion of families. This disorder behaves as an autosomal dominant trait, comprising non-insulin dependent diabetes, with onset in teenage or early adult life. There is genetic heterogeneity in this condition, with the other causative genes yet to be defined.

For children at risk of diabetes, awareness of risk rather than genetic testing seems most important at present. IDDM is likely to present rapidly with the typical features of lethargy, thirst, polyuria, and sometimes vomiting, but for those at risk of NIDDM, regular medical check ups in adult life, including testing for glycosuria or high blood sugar is important if early treatment is to prevent the onset of diabetic complications. A similar argument applies to MODY, although screening should commence at a younger age, and in those families with glucokinase mutations, DNA testing would be possible.

It can be seen that in some areas (eg. CATCH22) a common genetic aetiology has been discovered for a group of phenotypically similar disorders, whereas in other areas (long QT syndromes – cardiomyopathies, polycystic kidney disease, hyperlipidemias and diabetes) a multitude of genetic causes result in clinically similar conditions. Despite recent advances, there is much yet to unravel in the molecular genetics of cardiac disease and diabetes, and it is to be hoped that a better understanding of causes will lead to improvements in treatment. However, as genetic mechanisms are increasingly understood, and gene faults identified, so a whole new range of tests and screening possibilities may become available. In the adoption pre-placement, therefore, a family history of 'heart disease' or 'high blood pressure' may have far greater implications for investigation than is currently the case.

References

1 Nora J J, Berg K, Nora A H, *Cardiovascular diseases, Genetics, Epidemiology and Prevention*, Oxford University Press, 1991.

2 Shokeir M H K, 'Hypoplastic left heart: An autosomal recessive disorder', *Clinical Genetics*, 2:7-14, 1971.

3 Davidson H R, 'A large family with patent ductus arteriosus and unusual face', *Journal of Medical Genetics*, 30:503-505, 1992.

4 See 1 above.

5 Chiarella F, Bricarelli F D, Lupi G, Bellotti P, Domenicucci S, Vecchio C, 'Familial supravalvular aortic stenosis: a genetic study', *Journal of Medical Genetics*, 26:86-92 1989.

6 Ewart A K, Morris C A, Atkinson D, Weishan J, Sternes K, Spallone P, Stock A D, Leppert M, Keating M T, 'Hemizygosity at the elastin locus in a developmental disorder, Williams syndrome', *Nature Genetics*, 5:11-16, 1989.

7 Hall J G, 'CATCH22', *Journal of Medical Genetics*, 30:801-802, 1993.

8 See 1 above.

9 Jamieson C R, van der Burgt I, Brady A F, van Reen M, Elsawi M M, Hol F, Jeffery S, Patton M A, Mariman E, 'Mapping of a gene for Noonan syndrome to the long arm of chromosome 12', *Nature Genetics*, 8:357-360, 1994.

10 Turnpenny P D, Dean J C S, Auchterlonie I A, Johnston A W, 'Cardiofaciocutaneous syndrome with new ectodermal manifestations', *Journal of Medical Genetics*, 29:428-429, 1992.

11 Davies S J, Hughes H E, 'Costello syndrome: natural history and differential diagnosis of cutis laxa', *Journal of Medical Genetics*, 31:486-489, 1994.

12 See 1 above.

13 See 7 above.

14 Greenberg F, 'DiGeorge syndrome: an historical review of clinical and cytogenetic features', *Journal of Medical Genetics*, 30:803-806, 1992.

15 Wilson D I, Britton S B, McKeown C, Kelly D, Cross I E, Strobel S, Scambler P J, 'Noonan's and DiGeorge syndromes with monosomy 22q11', *Archives*

of Diseases in Childhood, 68:187-189, 1993.

16 Kelly D, Goldberg R, Wilson D, Lindsay E, Carey A, Goodship J, Burn J, Cross I, Shprintzen R J, Scambler P J, 'Confirmation that the velo-cardio-facial syndrome is associated with haplo-insufficiency of genes at chromosome 22q11', *American Journal of Medical Genetics*, 45:308-312, 1993, USA.

17 Wilson D I, Goodship J A, Burn J, Cross I E, Scambler P J, 'Deletions within chromsome 22q11 in familial congenital heart disease', *Lancet*, 340:573-575 13, 1992.

18 Halford S, Wadey R, Roberts C, Daw S C M, Whiting J A, O'Donnel H, Dunham I, Bentley D, Lindsay E, Baldini A, Francis F, Lehrach H, Williamson R, Wilson D I, Goodship J, Cross I, Burn J, Scambler P J, 'Isolation of a putative transcriptional regulator from the region of 22q11 deleted in DiGeorge syndrome and familial congenital heart disease', *Human Molecular Genetics*, 12:2099-2107, 1993.

19 See 6 above.

20 Lin A E, Chin A J, Devine W, Park S C, Zackai E, 'The pattern of cardiovascular malformation in the CHARGE association', *American Journal of Diseases in Childhood*, 141:1010-1013, 1987, USA.

21 See 1 above.

22 Pyeritz R E, McKusick V A, 'The Marfan syndrome: diagnosis and management', *New England Journal of Medicine*, 300:772-777, 1979, USA.

23 Gott V L, Pyertitz R E, Cameron D E, Greene P S, McKusick V A, 'Composite graft repair of Marfan aneurysm of the ascending aorta: results in 100 patients', *Ann Thorac Surgery* 52:38-45, 1991.

24 Shores J, Berger K R, Murphy E A, Pyeritz R E, 'Progression of aortic dilatation and the benefit of long-term Beta-adrenergic blockade in Marfan's syndrome', *New England Journal of Medicine*, 330:1335-1341, 1994, USA.

25 Kainulainen K, Pulkkinen L, Savolainen A, Kaitila I, Peltonen L, 'Location on chromosome 15 of the gene defect causing Marfan syndrome', *New England Journal of Medicine*, 323:935-939, 1990, USA.

26 Francke U, Furthmayr H, 'Marfan's syndrome and other disorders of fibrillin, *New England Journal of Medicine*, 330:1394-1385, 1994, USA.

27 Collod G, Babron M-C, Jondeau G, Coulon M, Weissenbach J, Dubourg O, Bourdarias J-P, Bonaïti-Pellié C, Junien C, Boileau C, 'A second locus for Marfan syndrome maps to chromosome 3 p24.2-p25', *Nature Genetics*, 8:264-268, 1994.

28 Pope F M, Kendall B E, Slapak G I, Kapoor R, McDonald W, Compston D A S, Mitchell R, Hope D T, Millar-Graig M W, Dean J C S, Johnston A W, Lynch P G, Sarathchandra P, Narcisi P, Nicholls A C, Richards A J, Mackenzie J L, 'Type III collagen mutations cause fragile cerebral arteries', *British Journal of Neurosurgery*, 5:551-574, 1991.

29 Kimberling W J, Fain P R, Kenyon J B, Godgan D, Sujansky E, Gabow P A, 'Linkage heterogeneity of autosomal dominant polycystic kidney disease', *New England Journal of Medicine*, 319:913-918, 1988, USA.

30 Bear J C, McManamon P, Morgan J, 'Age at clinical onset and at ultrasonographic detection of adult polycystic kidney disease. Data for genetic counselling', *American Journal of Medical Genetics*, 18:34-53, 1984, USA.

31 Editorial, 'Prime suspect for cystic kidneys', *Nature Genetics*, 7:341-42, 1994.

32 Gilligan D M, Cleland J G F, Oakley C M, 'The genetics of hypertrophic cardiomyopathy', *British Heart Journal*, 66:193-195,1991.

33 Solomon S D, Jarcho J A, McKenna W, Geisterfer-Lowrance A, Germain R, Salerni R, Seidman J, Seidman C E, 'Familial hypertrophic cardiomyopathy is a genetically heterogeneous disease', *Journal of Clinical Investigations*, 86:993-999, 1990.

34 Moolman J C, Brink P A, Corfield V A, 'Identification of a new missense mutation at Arg403, a CpG mutation hotspot, in exon 13 of the Beta-myosin heavy chain gene in hypertrophic cardiomyopathy', *Human Molecular Genetics*, 2:1731-32, 1993.

35 Gardner R J M, Hanson J W, Ionasescu V V, Ardinger H H, Skorton D J, Mahomey L T, Hart M N, Rose E F, Smith W L, Florentine M S, Hinrichs R L, 'Dominantly inherited dilated cardiomyopathy', *American Journal of Medical Genetics*, 27:61-73, 1987, USA.

36 Towbin J A, Hejtmancik J F, Brink P, Gelb B, Zhu X M, Chamberlain J S, McCabe ERB, Swift M, 'X-linked dilated cardiomyopathy', *Circulation*, 87:1854-1865, 1993.

37 Suomalainen A, Paetau A, Leinonen H, Majander A, Peltonen L, Somer H, 'Inherited idiopathic dilated cardiomyopathy with multiple deletions of mitochondrial DNA', *Lancet*, 340:1319-1320, 1992.

38 Swales J D, 'ACE gene: the plot thickens', *Lancet*, 342:1065, 1993.

39 See 1 above.

40 Vidaillet H J, Pressley J C, Henke E, Harrell F E, German L D, 'Familial occurrence of accessory atrioventricular pathways (pre-excitation syndrome)', *New England Journal of Medicine*, 317:65-69, 1993, USA.

41 Dean J C S, Cross S, Jennings K, 'Evidence of genetic and phenotypic heterogeneity in Romano-Ward syndrome', *Journal of Medical Genetics*, 30:947-950, 1993.

42 Jiang C, Atkinson D, Towbin J A, Splawski I, Lehmann M H, Li H, Timothy K, Taggart R T, Schwartz P J, Vincent G M, Moss A J, Keating M T, 'Two long QT syndrome loci map to chromosomes 3 and 7 with evidence for further heterogeneity', *Nature Genetics*, 8:141-147, 1994.

43 Williams R R, Hunt S C, Hasstedt S J, Hopkins P N, Wu L L, Berry T D, Stults B M, Barlow G K, Schumacher M C, Lifton R P, Lalouel J M, 'Multigenic human hypertension: evidence for subtypes and hope for haplotypes', *Journal of Hypertension*, 8(suppl 7): S39-S46, 1990.

44 Harrap S B, 'Hypertension: genes versus environment', *Lancet*, 344:169-171 35, 1994.

45 Gordon R D, Klemm S A, Tunny T J, Stowasser M, 'Primary aldosteronism: hypertension with a genetic basis', *Lancet* 340:159-161, 1992.

46 Berg K, 'Predictive genetic testing to control coronary heart disease and hyperlipidemia', *Arteriosclerosis Supplement 1*, 9:150-158, 1989.

47 Thompson G R, 'Lipids and the cardiovascular system', *Medicine International*, 31:373- 376, 1993.

48 Barnett A H, 'Genetics of type 1 diabetes mellitus', *British Journal of Hospital Medicine*, 47:513-517, 1992.

49 Bingley P J, Gale E A M, 'Aetiology and pathology of diabetes', *Medicine International*, 21:239-241, 1993.

50 See 46 above.

51 Editorial, 'Genetic basis of NIDDM', *Lancet*, 340:455-456, 1992.

11 The future of genetics in medicine and society

Dr Neva Haites

This chapter focuses on the rapid advances made in recent years in the study of genetics. It identifies key areas of research that scientists are currently involved in and also considers the application of genetic technologies to the understanding of some common disorders. It then considers the potential for treatment and therapeutic strategies in the future and discusses the ethics of gene therapy, including the safety, social and ethical issues involved as well as the legislation that permits, as well as restricts, access to confidential information.

Much attention has recently been focused on the rapid advances in molecular genetics and their application to improve our understanding of human development and disease. Projects have been funded to 'map' the genes and to determine the sequence of the entire human and mouse genome, that is, the complete set of genes.[1] These have captured the attention of researchers and politicians and have thus gained exposure in both the scientific and the popular press causing a higher level of awareness and increased expectations in patients. To facilitate this work, the USA and the EC have launched specifically funded 'Human Genome' projects. As a consequence, debate about the short and long-term consequences of this work for the problems of human health, the social and ethical issues involved, and the underlying science is developing.[2]

As the technology to study genomes and the function of genes expands, the question today is not whether the genes of humans and other higher organisms can be accurately placed on linear maps, but how rapidly the task will be completed; and equally, how quickly that knowledge can be applied to elucidate the molecular and cellular consequences of defects in these genes. Mapping or even sequencing can only tell us about gene content and position. A full biological understanding of disease processes requires a detailed knowledge of the controls which act on the genes and the function of their products. If this research is to improve our understanding of disease, we will require additional knowledge not only of the mutations which alter genes but of the means by which these disrupt the function of cellular processes.

No matter what path the genetic revolution takes, the first step is to find the genes: the discrete segments of DNA that are the basic units of inheritance. Each gene, of which there are at least 100,000, is encoded on one of 23 pairs of chromosomes in the human somatic cell. Each separate gene is composed of a series of 'three-letter words' or codons which are in turn made up of four possible molecular 'letters' called nucleotides. For instance, three copies of the chemical Uracil(U) appropriately linked in a row, UUU, codes for the amino acid, phenylalanine.

For scientists racing to map the human genome, 1993-94 have been very productive years. With automated cloning equipment and rough computerised maps to steer them through the vast stretches of DNA, scientists are finding human genes at the rate of more than one a day. In the past 12 months they have located many genes for inherited diseases including that for a common kind of colon cancer. Scientists have recently isolated the first breast cancer gene.

Human genome mapping projects

The UK Human Genome Mapping Project has two closely related and complementary arms.[3] One is a directed programme of work supported by grants and awards to the Medical Research Council (MRC) establishments and to university departments and independent institutions. The other is a Resource Centre which has three roles: to provide specialised services to the community; to collect, store, maintain and distribute reagents, materials and data, generated in the community; and to carry out sustained and systematic programmes of data generation. The Centre does not formally have research programmes of its own, but networks of collaborations are being set up to link its activities with research laboratories. Anyone with an interest in mapping the human genome can register as a user of the Resource Centre.

The European Community Human Genome Analysis Programme is just one component in a substantial portfolio of European centred work.

Phases of the programme have included the areas of research listed in Table 1.[4]

Table 1

Area of research

− Improvement of the human genetic map
− Physical mapping
− Improvements of the methods and basis for the study of the human genome
− DNA sequencing
− Technology development and applications of human genome analysis
− Data handling and databases
− Training fellowships
− Ethical, social and legal aspects of human genome mapping
− The programme is largely implemented by shared cost contracts awarded for research projects, but other forms of support include concerted action contracts, support for centralised facilities, bursaries and grants.

Scientists involved in these projects are now routinely producing information that exists at the sub microscopic level within every cell of the human body. Eventually the sequence of the chemical bases which make up the DNA chains in each of our 24 chromosomes (22 numbered pairs, or autosomes, plus an X and a Y) will be known. As in most other areas of biological science, genetics crosses species barriers. The nature of the nucleic acid sequence coding for the composition of a gene's protein product are common to the most simple and the most complex forms of life. Experiments on the actions of specific genes to determine somatic development in the fruit fly, or a primitive nematode worm (*Caenorhabditis elegnas*) have been found to have counterparts in higher organisms. Techniques for physical mapping of the genome of the nematode has allowed the development of technologies required for large-scale sequencing, pointing the way to a similar more complex exercise in humans.[5]

The genetic constitution and even the map of the mouse and a human being are surprisingly similar, and as a result, the study of similarity between species (homology) is a valuable way of learning about human genetics. A team in Oxford has focused on the identification and utilisation of sequences in the mouse genome, known as microsatellites, which consist of long arrays of dinucleotide repeats. The size of these repeats shows great variation even between inbred strains and these serve as very useful tools in the mapping of genes.[6]

Many vehicles are utilised for the preparation of purified genes (called gene cloning). These include viruses, bacteria and yeast. The recently developed technique of transgenesis, which enables, for example, a disease causing human mutation to be replicated in the mouse, or a normal gene to be placed in a diseased animal, is opening new ways of studying the interactive effect of human genes and are a means of developing and testing novel means of therapeutic intervention. Several transgenic animals have now been developed. These include both the 'Cystic Fibrosis' mouse and the 'p53 knock out' mouse which are likely to provide ideal means of studying the safety and appropriate timing of new forms of therapy in both cases and the relationship of the p53 gene to cancer development in the latter.[7,8,9]

Advances to date

It is remarkable that, over a period of less than ten years, the genes responsible for virtually all of the relatively common inherited diseases have been mapped, isolated by cloning, and disease causing mutations characterised. For an ever increasing list of diseases the defective gene product is now known as a direct result of identification (by positional cloning) of the defective gene. For example, Duchenne muscular dystrophy, an X-linked condition which is ultimately fatal in affected males, is characterised by progressive weakness and wasting. The gene, which is defective in such boys, codes for a protein called 'dystrophin'.[10] This protein is now known to be involved in providing the muscle cell with the necessary strength and resilience to withstand constant contractions and relaxations. In its absence muscle cells break down and are replaced by fatty, fibrous tissue. From our knowledge of the gene involved, it is now possible to provide accurate carrier detection and prenatal diagnosis if requested by the parents. The majority of disease specific mutations are deletions, ie. where small pieces of the gene are missing. The same gene is also involved in causing the milder, adult form of Becker Muscular dystrophy.[11] With this knowledge, several strategies are now being studied for possible therapeutic intervention.

Similarly, genes have been identified for other autosomal diseases. Cystic fibrosis, one of the commonest fatal diseases in the Caucasian population, has been shown to be due to a gene which codes for a membrane protein involved in the transport of ions across the cell membrane.[12] When a mutant protein is produced, this movement of ions is compromised and as a result the extracellular fluids, including the mucous in the lungs, is thicker and infection develops behind blocked airways. As mentioned above, a mouse model of this disease has been developed and as we will see in the next section, 'gene therapy' is already being tested in both animal models and in affected patients.

A large number of other inherited diseases have similarly been successfully studied and include those listed in Table 2.[13]

Table 2

Disease	Gene	Function
Haemophilia A	Factor VIII	coagulation
Haemophilia B	Factor IX	coagulation
Huntington disease	Huntington	unknown
Fragile X mental retardation	FraX A	unknown
Familial adenomatous polyposis coli	APC	Tumour suppressor
Marfan's syndrome	fibrillin 15	strength of connective tissue
HMSN 1A	PMP22	myelin protein
Motor neurone disease	SOD1	inhibits oxidative damage
MEN1A	RET	oncogene/tyrosine kinase
Hirschsprung's disease	RET	oncogene/adhesion

The genetic technologies can also be applied to understanding some of the more common disorders which have a genetic background but which are not simply inherited. While this is more difficult, it is of enormous potential benefit. The disorders in question include: cardiovascular disease, common cancers, diabetes, the major psychoses, and many congenital malformations. Reports have appeared identifying single genes which play a major role in causing some of these disorders.

These studies suggest that several different genes and interactions with the environment are involved in many diseases, and the particular one which plays a critical role in one family may not make the same contribution in the next family. These studies are perhaps of greater significance to the practice of medicine in the future, and will provide information on the molecular aspects of many potentially multifactorial diseases. For example, the study of cancer genetics has been facilitated by the presence of many inherited forms of cancer. Although these forms are rare, they have been found to be a model for many of the sporadic forms of cancer with the molecular events involved in the predisposition in such families being one of the commonest molecular events in the comparable sporadic form.

Thus, although familial adenomatous polyposis coli only accounts for one per cent of colon cancer,[14] the gene which is mutant in the germ line of such cases, the adenomatous polyposis coli gene (APC) is also found to be commonly mutated in sporadic colon cancer. One of the most common molecular events found in all solid tumours is in the p53 tumour suppressor gene for which a knock out mouse model has been developed. Again, a very rare form of inherited predisposition to cancer, the Li-Fraumeni syndrome, has been found to be due to an inherited mutation in the p53 tumour suppressor gene.[15]

The stimulus provided by the Human Genome Mapping Project has raised the profile of clinical and molecular genetics in the UK providing the means for recruiting able young graduates into this area of medical research. To capitalise, we must now move in several directions. There are immediate clinical applications in diagnosis, carrier detection, and prenatal diagnosis of single gene inherited diseases. Transfer of information and reagents from the research laboratory to the clinical service laboratory has been rapid in this field with clinical diagnosis often being made long before research is formally published.

Treatment

As our understanding of the molecular events involved in disease improves so does our ability to design logical therapeutic strategies. These can include the production of normal factors missing in the disease state for use in replacement, eg. human factor VIII can be produced in lower organisms for the treatment of haemophiliacs as can human insulin. The use of human products for replacement therapies must generally be superior to the use of animal substitutes. Much careful laboratory work has shown how genes, artificially inserted into cultured cells, can correct inherent genetic defects, even for quite complex disorders such as cystic fibrosis and Duchenne muscular dystrophy (DMD).[16,17,18]

The first patients to receive 'gene therapy', the insertion of a functional gene into cells which are then introduced into patients, are being carefully monitored. Progress has been so rapid that gene therapy for a number of simple inherited disorders is now available in certain centres and trials have begun for others.

The first clinical trials began in 1993 in the UK when doctors at Great Ormond Street Hospital, in collaboration with colleagues in the Netherlands, took bone marrow from a child with severe combined immunodeficiency caused by the inheritance of two copies (one from each parent) of a defective gene for the enzyme, adenosine deaminase. These doctors introduced a normal copy of the gene into the bone marrow cells from the child, using a disabled retrovirus, and then returned them to the child. In the USA, at least four children have received similar therapy for this condition and for the first two treated in this way, the last three years since the treatment began has allowed them to return to a near normal existence.[19,20]

In 1992, the Clothier committee reported on the ethics of gene therapy in the UK and found that for somatic gene therapy (in which the genes are targeted to the cells of specific affected organs and not to the egg or sperm cells) there were no major substantial ethical issues.[21] As a result, gene therapy for three major classes of disease have begun to be studied. These include the single gene disorders which are largely recessive in inheritance, the inherited defects in metabolism, and cancer. Listed in Table 3 are some of the trials that are underway in the UK and USA.[22,23,24]

As mentioned above, the potential to develop gene therapy for other single gene disorders has been greatly facilitated by the development of transgenic animal models. Several groups of researchers have disrupted the CFTR gene (which when mutant causes cystic fibrosis) in mouse embryonic stem cells and have bred mice which are carrying two mutant copies of the gene. These mice have many of the symptoms of children with the disease. Recently, scientists in Oxford and Cambridge have shown that when copies of the normal CFTR genes were introduced into the lungs of these mice by using chemical vehicles called cationic liposomes, the defect is corrected in some cases. In the USA and UK, trials are now underway using adenoviruses and liposomes to carry the normal copy of the gene initially into the nasal passages and later the lungs of individuals affected with cystic fibrosis.

Table 3

Disease	Therapy
Cystic fibrosis	adenovirus containing CFTR liposome containing CFTR
Severe combined immunodeficiency disease (SCID)	retrovirus containing adenosine deaminase
Familial hypercholesterolaemia	LDL receptor
Duchenne muscular dystrophy	Dystrophin
Cancer	Interleukins; thymidine kinase; tumour suppressor genes.

Safety issues
As with any rapidly developing science, it is essential that appropriate regulations are introduced and monitored to ensure that research is carried out within carefully considered guidelines. Naturally, a proportion of the population has fears relating to the potential for harm caused by the new genetic technologies. Some of these fears have a sound basis and will be considered by the appropriate regulatory bodies who must give approval

for all work involving, for example, DNA manipulation or gene therapy. In the USA and the UK, as in other European countries, committees have been constituted to lay down guidelines and to plan for any necessary legislation to ensure that all work of this nature carried out in their countries is done within strict safety guidelines which are suitably monitored.

All future developments should be discussed and openly debated by both the general public and by professionals. In many countries this is difficult due to the poor state of education of the public regarding science in general and genetics in particular. It is therefore essential that education of the population continues and that this should be broader than the current tendency of some media presentations to highlight the sensational and the potential for misuse.[25,26]

Social and ethical issues

As a result of many of these advances important social and ethical issues need to be considered and debated by society. For example, the rights of an individual whose genetic make up holds important information which may be relevant to a close relative; the relative rights of insurer and insured to the genetic information which may predict illness in the insured; and other issues which need to be carefully considered and decided by society and its representatives – not by scientists and doctors alone. It is likely that sensible informed discussion in conjunction with education will, over a period of time, produce a general social consensus on these matters. Certainly, the potential for improvement in human health and for the prevention of suffering by the application of information on the basic biological processes which determine our development and function is as important and challenging a goal as has ever faced medical science.

The concern about the resurgence of eugenic policies in small and large communities needs to be fully aired. The opinions and policies of previous generations of professionals and politicians has made it imperative that today's 'new genetics' be carefully monitored to identify and limit any recurrence of potential problems. It would be foolish to consider that no genetic discrimination could occur today. Numerous examples of genetic discrimination directed against individuals or families based solely on their apparent or perceived genetic variation from the "normal" phenotype exist. These are manifest in many social institutions but especially in the health and insurance industries and are probably more of a problem in some countries than others.[27,28,29,30]

Data protection

In order to truly allow an individual to have free choice concerning who has access to their own, and their family's, genetic predisposition and medical history, it is essential that all records are protected from view to all excepting those specifically entitled.

The Access to Health Records Act came into force in November 1991 and allows patients the right of access to their own written health records. Computer held records have been accessible since the 1984 Data Protection Act. Patients also have the right to challenge what they believe to be inaccurate information. When it comes to genetic case notes, such a ruling is not as easy to comply with because, in general, such notes are for a family and hence will contain confidential information on a large number in individuals within the family, both living and dead.[31]

Similarly, computer registers of genetic cases containing family data will include information on many individuals both affected and unaffected and hence access to both these forms of information must be limited. For patient information to be stored on computer data bases, the registrar must be registered under the Data Protection Act.[32] Currently even clinical colleagues must obtain the consent of the Consultant Clinical Geneticist in charge of the family to have access to the genetic notes and often it is necessary to cull selected portions of the notes that refer to other individuals other than the patient in question.

Where third parties are mentioned in the notes, the Data Protection Act will require the doctor to withhold that information unless they have been given permission to pass it on by the patient. The BMA's Ethics Committee has produced guidelines on the Act which explain the implications and obligations for doctors under the legislation. These cover arrangements for access to records and safeguards for areas of concern including time limits.[33] The guidelines also cover third party access by parents or relatives on behalf of children or mentally incompetent patients.

Releasing the records of deceased patients to insurance companies has also been highlighted as a concern for doctors. The guidelines state that no information can be released if the patient has signed their records and requested non-disclosure of information or if they have given information to the doctor which, at the time, they have expected to remain confidential. This is in line with the BMA policy which states that doctors should not release any health information about deceased patients to insurance companies, regardless of whether or not the patients have signed their records.

Insurance

The question of whether companies that issue policies for health insurance, disability insurance, and life insurance should have access to the results of genetic tests could be addressed as a part of a more fundamental issue, the irreconcilable dilemma in underwriting. Tradition-ally, an insurance policy affords protection against very large costs resulting from the occurrence of an undesirable event whose probability is small. If the probability of loss is the same for each person then each will pay the same premium. But if the insurance company has information about the relative risks to each person it might charge premiums proportional to the risk.[34]

Solutions to this dilemma have been proposed and include a possible moratorium on the use of genetic information by insurance companies. However, if insurance premiums are set to be equal for all people then the phenomenon of adverse selection could arise with people at high risk tending to purchase a great deal of insurance while those at low risk might purchase less. As a result, insurance companies might be forced to raise their premiums to cover their expenses. On the other hand, if a company charges high premiums to those at high genetic risk (a small proportion of the total population but those most in need of insurance), the majority of these individuals will not be able to afford policies.

Conclusion

Rapid advances have been made and will continue to be made to our understanding of the basic biology of human disease. This will undoubtedly result in new and more specific forms of treatment. As this work progresses, issues will be raised which may cause concern to the population as a whole or may jeopardise an individual's rights. Fortunately, in the USA and Europe, policy-making bodies have been quick to establish broad-based committees which can establish clear guidelines. In addition, however, new laws may be needed to protect reproductive decision making, regulate access to genetic data banks and prohibit genetic discrimination.

As progress in human genetics is made, adopted individuals and others in the adoption circle may be particularly vulnerable. Crucial information about family medical history may be lacking, which may deny adopted individuals opportunities for predictive genetic testing on the one hand and expose them to greater discrimination, with respect to medical insurance, on the other.

References

1   Bobrow M, Introduction, *Medical Research Council News* No 53:4-5, 1991.

2   Annas G J, and Elias S, 'Legal and ethical implications for fetal diagnosis and gene therapy', *American Journal of Medical Genetics*, 35:215-218, 1990, USA.

3   Vickers T, 'The Resource Centre of the UK HGMP and Europe', *Medical Research Council News*, No 53:52-53, 1991.

4   See 3 above.

5   'The Genetic Revolution', *TIME*, No 3:32-42, January 1994, USA.

6   Copeland N G, et al, 'Development and application of a molecular genetic linkage map of the mouse genome', *Trends in Genetics*, 7:113-118, 1991.

7   Dorin J R, et al, 'Cystic fibrosis in the mouse by targeted insertional mutagenesis', *Nature*, 359:211-5, 1991.

8   Porteous D J, et al, 'Gene therapy for cystic fibrosis – where and when?' *Human Molecular Genetics*, 2:211-212, 1993.

9   Donehower L A, et al, 'Mice deficient for p53 are developmentally normal but susceptible to spontaneous tumours', *Nature*, 356:215-221, 1992.

10 Dunckley M G, et al, 'Direct retroviral-mediated transfer of a dystrophin

minigene into mdx mouse muscle in vivo', *Human Molecular Genetics*, 2(6):717-23, 1993.

11 Love D R, et al, 'Becker muscular dystrophy patient with a large intragenic dystrophin deletion: implications for functional minigenes and gene therapy', *Journal of Medical Genetics*, 28:860-864, 1991.

12 Hyde S C, et al, 'Correction of the ion transport defect in cystic fibrosis transgenic mice by gene therapy', *Nature*, 362:250-255, 1993.

13 Cooper D N, and Schmidtke J, 'Diagnosis of genetic disease using recombinant DNA', Third edition, *Human Genetics*, 87:519-569, 1991.

14 Groden J, et al, 'Identification and characterisation of the familial adenomatous polyposis coli gene', *Cell*, 66:589-600, 1991.

15 Coutelle C, et al, 'Gene therapy for cystic fibrosis', *Archives of Diseases in Childhood*, 68:437-43, 1993.

16 See 10 above.

17 See 12 above.

18 See 15 above.

19 Miller Dusty A, 'Human gene therapy comes of age', *Nature*, 357:455-460, 1992.

20 Davies K, and Williamson B, 'Gene therapy begins', *British Medical Journal*, 306:1625-1626, 1993.

21 Clothier C, *Report of the Committee on the Ethics of Gene Therapy*, London: HMSO, 1992.

22 Williamson R, 'From genome mapping to gene therapy', *Trends in Biotechnology*, 11:159-161, 1993.

23 Porteous D J, and Dorin J R, 'How relevant are mouse models for human diseases to somatic gene therapy?' *Trends in Biotechnology*, 11:173-181, 1993.

24 Gutierrez A A, et al, 'Gene therapy for cancer', *Lancet*, 339:715-21.6, 1992.

25 Harper P, 'Genetics and public health', *British Medical Journal*, 304:721, 1992.

26 Tonks A, 'Ethics committee demands control on genetic screening', *British Medical Journal*, 307:1513, 1993.

27 Holtzman N A, and Rothstein M A, 'Eugenics and genetic discrimination', *American Journal of Human Genetics*, 50:456-459, 1992.

28 Billings P R, et al, 'Discrimination as a consequence of genetic testing', *American Journal of Human Genetics*, 50:476-482, 1992.

29 Annas GJ, and Elias S, Legal and Ethical Implications of Fetal Diagnosis and gene therapy, *American Journal of Medical Genetics*, 35:215-218, 1990.

30 Nuffield Council on Bioethics, *Genetic screening: ethical issues*, Nuffield Council on Bioethics, 1993.

31 'Opening the records to patient scrutiny', *BMA News Review*, September 1991.

32 Knox E G, 'Confidential medical records and epidemiological research', *British Medical Journal*, 304:727-728, 1992.

33 See 31 above.

34 Alper J S, and Natowicz M R, 'Genetic testing and insurance', *British Medical Journal*, 307:1506-1507, 1993.

Section 3:
Testing, screening and the right to information

Genetic testing and screening, and the sharing of information from these investigations or enquiries, have become issues of vigorous debate in relation to the ethics of modern medicine, much encouraged by media interest. The issues are clearly a key area of concern within adoption, where special difficulties with respect to confidentiality exist, both legally and in practice. In this section we have attempted to cover the field of genetic testing and screening, and related ethical problems, as comprehensively as possible for a book of this kind.

The scene is set by a contribution (Chapter 12) outlining the concepts, rationale, and current availability of medical screening, and this is followed by three (Chapters 13 – 16) which explore psychological and ethical aspects from different perspectives. The first of these (Chapter 13) introduces the reader to the new discipline of 'psychosocial genetics', which is concerned with studying the personal impact of genetic testing as well as the implications for society in general. Secondly, it is most timely that the Clinical Genetics Society of the UK published their Working Party's Report on Genetic Testing in Children in 1994 as this provides a very helpful framework for adoption workers who face issues relating to such testing in adopted people. The report has been specially adapted for this publication because of its relevance and importance (Chapter 14). Lastly, confidentiality and disclosure of information are viewed from both medical and legal perspectives (Chapters 15 and 16). Seldom can it be claimed there are any absolute 'rules', as those involved in counselling will acknowledge, and much work is required if the medical and legal professions are to proceed in step with each other on these issues.

12 Screening for genetic disease

Dr Zofia Miedzybrodzka

This paper offers in-depth information about screening for genetic disease. It includes an explanation of what screening involves, discusses the benefits, considers the costs, and looks at the best way to offer screening. The second section of the paper provides a summary of the current availability of genetic screening in the UK. A helpful preface that explains the terminology used in the paper will guide the reader.

Terminology

In the medical context, *screening* is the systematic application of a test or inquiry, to identify individuals who are at sufficient risk of a specific disorder to benefit from further investigation or direct preventive action, among persons who have not sought medical attention on account of symptoms of that disorder.

Detection rate or *sensitivity* is how good a test is at detecting the problem it is looking for. The phrase *"false negative rate"* can be used to indicate the proportion of those affected by the problem that are not detected by the test. *Specificity* is a measure of how many people with a positive screening test will actually have the problem being looked for. The phrase *"false positive rate"* is sometimes used to complement the term *sensitivity*, meaning the proportion of individuals with positive screening tests who do not in fact have the condition being screened for.

What is targeted or population screening?

In targeted screening, a sub-group of the population is selected for testing, usually because people within that group are at higher risk of the condition being tested for. Two examples of targeted screening are the offer of genetic testing to relatives of people with adult polycystic kidney disease, and the offer of amniocentesis to pregnant women over the age of 37. Alternatively, the whole of a population may be screened, an example being "triple test" (a blood test) screening of pregnant women for Down's syndrome, regardless of their age.

Genetic screening tests

Tests may aim to identify individuals already affected by a disease (eg. cystic fibrosis in some areas), identify those who are at risk of developing a disease but are still unaffected by it (presymptomatic testing eg. testing for adult polycystic kidney disease before renal failure occurs so that blood pressure can be treated to slow the progression of the disease), or testing for asymptomatic carriers, who might pass on the condition to their children but are not affected themselves.

Tests can be done by looking at:
– genes themselves (mutation detection);
– genetic markers linked to a gene within a family with a particular condition (genetic linkage);
– chromosomes which are tested by using a karyotype from blood, amniotic fluid, chorionic villus or skin biopsy;
– markers of disease (eg. blood levels of the muscle protein creatine kinase to test for muscular dystrophies);
– signs of the disease (eg. ultrasound scanning to look for kidney cysts in polycystic kidney disease);
– the disease itself (eg. examination for congenital hip dislocation).
The different types of test may be used alone or in combination.

Benefits of screening

Benefits vary according to the type of screening. Screening for affected or pre-symptomatic cases of a disease is performed to improve outcome in those identified or to provide those individuals with information to make life decisions. For example, Guthrie card testing (a blood test offered to every five-day-old British baby (see below) prevents the complications caused by the treatable conditions, phenylketonuria (PKU) and congenital hypothyroidism. Untreated, both conditions cause mental retardation, with all its social costs for the sufferer and family. Although such screening is costly to organise and deliver, it actually saves the NHS money by preventing the need for long-term care. A very different example is that of Huntington's disease. Although there is no treatment currently available for those who have inherited an affected Huntington's disease gene, many individuals at risk of doing so choose to have a predictive test in order to plan their family and to know what they are facing in the future.

The purpose of screening for asymptomatic carriers (eg. for autosomal recessive disorders like cystic fibrosis or thalassaemia) is to increase reproductive choice. Those at risk may choose to have prenatal diagnosis with a view to termination of an affected foetus, may choose not to have further children, or merely be aware of their risks. In addition, tests may offer reassurance to those who test negative, although we must remember that most of those tested were unaware of the risk before the test was offered.

Costs of screening

Screening may raise anxiety, particularly for the bulk of screenees who test negative. False reassurance is a common side-effect, with many of those who have had negative results being unaware of the limitations of the test, and therefore their remaining risk.[1] In the early days of haemoglobinopathy screening in Greece, detected carriers were socially stigmatised, and deemed only fit to marry other carriers![2] This was the exact opposite of the aim of the screening programme, which encouraged carriers to marry non-carriers. Better population education has solved this problem but the lesson must be remembered. Prenatal screening to test for Down's syndrome has been shown to change mothers' attitudes to pregnancy and their babies.[3]

It is important to remember that prenatal diagnosis carries a risk of miscarriage (up to 3-4 per cent for chorionic villus sampling (CVS), 0.5-1 per cent for amniocentesis), and the babies lost through miscarriage are likely to be unaffected by the condition being tested for.

With the heavy costs of population screening, full evaluation of new screening programmes is particularly important, as they may remove resources from other more deserving areas of health care. Such decisions must be made in the light of all costs and benefits, not merely the financial ones.

The best way to offer screening

Moderating the unwanted effects of screening
Many of the undesirable effects of screening can be moderated by inviting

patients to participate, preparing those who undergo testing and giving negative as well as positive results.[4] Explaining why an individual is being invited – even if it is a routine request – is useful; some women misinterpret an invitation to attend for cervical screening as evidence that it is thought likely that they have cancer.[5] Information given before the test should include what the test is and is not for, how the test will be carried out, when and how the results are given, the likelihood of being recalled and the meaning of positive and negative results. It is known that health professionals consistently underestimate the amount of information that patients want.[6] Negative results are generally reassuring but greater benefit is derived if results are communicated, rather than women being told to assume that no news is good news.[7] A consultation for a positive result should include attention to the patient's concerns as well as instituting further investigation.

Education of health providers (physicians, nursing staff, etc.) is also necessary if screening programmes are to be provided uniformly and well but staff training is often neglected.[8] A Montréal study of Tay-Sachs heterozygote screening found that the physician was "the most powerful potential advocate of screening".[9] Fifteen years later a study of Tay-Sachs screening referrals in New York State found that although the consensus was that pre-conception screening was preferable, most referrals were from obstetricians in pregnancy, not from internists and family physicians pre-pregnancy.[10]

Timing of screening

Screening may be offered at any time from birth to adult life, either systematically or opportunistically. The best time for screening varies between screening programmes. For example, screening for affected individuals with cystic fibrosis or muscular dystrophy must be done within early life to be worthwhile. However, testing neonates or children for carrier status or presymptomatic disease prevents them from making their own choice to have that knowledge, and may not seem relevant to an individual at a time in their lives when the result is not important. In addition, retention of results and their meaning may be poor. Preconception carrier testing allows couples to come to terms with their risk and to avoid pregnancy, whereas pregnant women have a high degree of interest in their own reproduction, and have usually chosen their partner and are readily available for counselling by specialised staff.

Experience with thalassaemia screening suggests that many couples will not present for screening before pregnancy, while others will forget their carrier status; so antenatal screening is always required.[11] Furthermore, the opportunity for preconception screening is limited by the large number of pregnancies that are unplanned. A survey of recent parents found that 50 per cent favoured cystic fibrosis carrier testing in pregnancy, 34 per cent thought testing school leavers to be best, and only 13 per cent chose testing of non-pregnant prospective parents.[12]

Current availability of genetic screening in the UK

1. Population screening widely available within the UK
Neonatal screening

All children born in the UK are medically examined within the first few days of life. Special attention is paid to the detection of remediable conditions like congenital dislocation of the hip. In addition, every child born in the UK has a Guthrie test on the fifth day of life. Five drops of blood from a heel prick are spotted onto a card and allowed to dry before being sent to a central laboratory for testing. The actual tests performed on the blood sample vary between areas but tests for phenylketonuria (PKU) and congenital hypothyroidism are routine everywhere. Other disorders that may be tested for include galactosaemia and maple syrup urine disease, and rarely, diagnostic (not carrier) tests for cystic fibrosis or Duchenne muscular dystrophy.

1. *Phenylketonuria (PKU; autosomal recessive):* PKU is caused by an inability to metabolise the amino acid phenylalanine. If PKU is detected and treated early by a diet low in phenylalanine, the mental retardation caused by this condition can be avoided. Few physical signs of the condition are present before brain damage occurs, so population screening is the only way to identify affected children early enough for treatment to be fully effective. Testing is performed by measuring blood phenylalanine in the dried blood spot. False negatives (affected cases not detected) are rare, and families with affected children can be offered

genetic counselling. About one in 10,000 UK babies are born with PKU.

2. *Congenital hypothyroidism:* Congenital hypothyroidism is generally sporadic, but occasionally autosomal recessive. Early diagnosis and therapy permits normal development, but few signs are present in the newborn. Untreated, it causes mental retardation (cretinism). About one in 4,000 babies are born with congenital hypothyroidism.

Prenatal screening
Routine antenatal care offers the following genetic screening tests at many centres. The individual tests offered vary widely between hospitals.

1. *Family history of genetic disease* is enquired about and appropriate genetic referral can be arranged. Although it is best for such tests to be done before pregnancy to allow sufficient time for complicated tests to take place, and for family history to be confirmed, many couples do not present for testing before pregnancy.

2. *Down's syndrome* is the commonest form of mental retardation, most often caused by each cell having three copies of chromosome 21. Chromosome abnormalities can be detected prenatally by amniocentesis. As women get older, their risk of having an affected child increases. Thus, in some centres, a diagnostic amniocentesis test is offered to all women over the age of 35 (or 37). At these ages the risk of Down's syndrome is similar to that of the amniocentesis itself (0.5–1 per cent miscarriage rate). Amniocentesis can also detect other chromosome abnormalities, some of which will be serious, others unimportant, and some of uncertain importance.

However, this type of screening leaves most cases of Down's syndrome undetected. Most babies are born to women under the age of 35, so although the risk is lower for each individual younger mother, most babies with Down's syndrome are born to younger mothers. The risk of miscarriage following amniocentesis, let alone the cost of the procedure, means that amniocentesis is not a suitable screening test for the younger population. Therefore, a blood test was developed to select women for amniocentesis. The blood levels of the pregnancy proteins alphafetoprotein (AFP), human chorionic gonadotrophin (HCG) and sometimes oestriol, are measured at 16 weeks gestation. A computer combines the blood test results with maternal age to calculate the risk that the pregnancy is affected by Down's syndrome. If the calculated risk of the foetus being affected is greater than a cut off level (usually arbitrarily decided as about one in 250 or one in 280), amniocentesis is offered. As the majority of babies will be normal, the psychological costs of such testing must not be underrated, although most pregnant women still value the opportunity for testing. Unfortunately, this test only detects 50-60 per cent of cases, so some women who would have been offered amniocentesis on the basis of age alone still choose to have a diagnostic amniocentesis.[13,14]

The test is known by various names including triple testing, double testing, maternal serum screening and the Down's syndrome/spina bifida test. It is not available in all parts of the UK.

3. Anencephaly and spina bifida: The age/AFP/HCG test (triple test) also tests for risk of anencephaly and spina bifida (neural tube defects), by looking at the level of AFP. Some areas test maternal serum samples for AFP alone, instead of performing the triple test. Mothers whose risk of having an affected foetus is greater than about one in 200 (cut-off levels vary) are offered diagnostic testing. Detailed ultrasound scans and sometimes amniocentesis are used as diagnostic tests, but only about 5 per cent of women who screen positive have affected fetuses. The test detects about 80 per cent of spina bifida and most cases of anencephaly. Neural tube defects are usually sporadic, although relatives of an affected child/foetus are at increased risk of having an affected child themselves and some autosomal recessive forms exist.

4. Foetal ultrasound: Ultrasound scanning is used widely for dating pregnancies and detecting multiple pregnancies. It is becoming used increasingly in pregnancy to detect fetal abnormality, some of which may be genetic, especially by a detailed scan at 18 weeks. This can detect spina bifida, some renal and heart abnormalities and point to diagnosis of some chromosome abnormalities. Other diagnostic tests like amniocentesis may also be performed.

2. Targeted screening

The following types of test are available through NHS clinical genetics services at the request of the general practitioner. Some may also be performed by other services, eg. antenatal clinics.

Family history of genetic disease

In most areas of the UK, genetic counselling and appropriate genetic tests are available for individuals with a family history of genetic disease. Consultands are usually encouraged to inform their relatives of genetic risk and the availability of testing. Examples of diseases commonly screened for include familial adenomatous polyposis coli (multiple potentially cancerous polyps develop in the colon, but prophylactic surgery can prevent early death from malignancy), and adult polycystic kidney disease (early treatment of hypertension and diet may prolong renal function).

Cystic fibrosis (CF)

CF carrier testing is widely available for relatives of individuals with CF. Such testing is encouraged by some CF clinics, but must still be done with appropriate counselling. Although recent advances in treatment allow survival for a mean of about 25 years, CF is a debilitating disease with far reaching social consequences.

Sickle cell disease

Carriers can be offered genetic counselling and anaesthetic risk is identified, allowing better monitoring to take place. Affected individuals suffer severe chronic haemolytic anaemia and painful "crises" with blood clotting secondary to the abnormally shaped blood cells causing pain and sometimes loss of function. Infections of bone and lung are common. Life span is still shortened despite modern management.

Tay-Sachs disease

Although screening is not offered on a systematic basis in the UK for Tay-Sachs disease, testing is available through genetic centres. In some areas, a more systematic approach is used, in others the Jewish population have organised their own anonymous screening programme. One in 30

Ashkenazi Jews carry the Tay-Sachs disease gene compared to 1 in 300 non-Jews, thus one in 3,600 Jewish births are affected. Carrier testing is done using a biochemical assay and prenatal diagnosis is possible by CVS. Affected children have progressive neurological abnormalities from late infancy, and die within 3-4 years.

The Jewish community testing programmes have modified the role of the traditional matchmaker. That individual (usually a rabbi) oversees marriages by arranging the testing of prospective partners for Tay-Sachs disease and cystic fibrosis (Ian Ellis, personal communication) and would call off the marriage if both individuals were carriers of the same defective gene.

Future possibilities for screening

Cystic fibrosis carrier screening

Cystic fibrosis (CF) is the commonest life threatening autosomal recessive disease in the British population, affecting one in 2,500 of the population. One in 25 individuals are asymptomatic carriers, 80-90 per cent of whom can be identified by a simple mouthwash test (mutation detection). CF causes chronic lung disease, pancreatic insufficiency and a number of other complications. Despite new treatments CF still shortens life. Current median survival is 25 years, although those benefiting from today's therapy will probably live longer, and gene therapy may one day provide some type of cure. Pilot studies of CF carrier screening have been performed in the UK, testing adults pre-pregnancy and at antenatal clinics. Uptake of screening is low in pre-pregnancy (varying between 10 per cent and 60 per cent depending how the test is offered), but 80-90 per cent of those offered tests at antenatal clinics accept. The results of long-term follow up studies are required to assess the true benefits and costs of such screening. Screening is available on the NHS in two areas where pilot studies were performed, although several research studies are ongoing. However, CF screening is expensive and thus may not be widely implemented.

Other possibilities for UK population screening might be to search for Fragile X carriers and genetic predisposition to common cancers. As with all screening programmes, full evaluation of the feasibility and psychological and economic aspects are required before a screening programme becomes widespread practice.

References

1 Marteau T M, 'Psychological costs of screening', *British Medical Journal*, 299:527, 1989.

2 Stamatoyannopoulos G, 'Problems of screening and counselling in the haemoglobinopathies', *Birth defects: proceedings of the fourth international conference*, (eds) Motulsky A G, and Ebling F J G, *Excerpta Medica*, 268-276, 1974.

3 Marteau T M, Johnston M, Shaw R W, Michie S, Kidd J, and New M, 'The impact of prenatal screening and diagnostic testing upon the cognitions, emotions and behaviour of pregnant women', *J Psychosom Res*, 33:7-16, 1989.

4 Marteau T M, 'Screening in Practice: Reducing the psychological costs', *British Medical Journal*, 301:26-28, 1990.

5 Nathoo V, 'Investigation of non-responders at a cervical cancer screening clinic in Manchester', *British Medical Journal*, 296:1041-1042, 1988.

6 Marteau T M, 'Ethics of clinical research', *British Medical Journal*, 299:513-514, 1989.

7 See 4 above.

8 See 4 above.

9 Beck E, Blaichman S, Scriver C R and Clow, C L, 'Advocacy and compliance in genetic screening', *New England Journal of Medicine*, 291:1166-1170, 1974, USA.

10 Shapiro D A, and Shapiro L R, 'Pitfalls in Tay-Sachs carrier detection: Physician referral patterns and patient ignorance', *NY State Journal of Medicine*, 89:317-319, 1989, USA.

11 Modell B, 'Cystic fibrosis screening and community genetics', *Journal of Medical Genetics*, 27:475-479, 1990.

12 Green J M, 'Principles and practicalities of carrier screening: attitudes of

recent parents', *Journal of Medical Genetics*, 29:313-319, 1992.

13 Wald N, et al, 'Antenatal maternal serum screening for Down's syndrome: results of a demonstration project', *British Medical Journal*, 305:391-394, 1993.

14 Marteau T M, 'Psychological consequences of screening for Down's syndrome', *British Medical Journal*, 307:146-147, 1993.

13 Knowing too much or knowing too little
Psychological questions raised for the adoption process by genetic testing

Dr Susan Michie and Dr Theresa Marteau

Advances in genetics present opportunities to determine the risk of disease to oneself, and to one's future children. The majority of tests are offered on the basis of a high risk indicated by a history of disease within one's biological family.

These prospects have implications for everyone, affecting how we view health, pregnancy, children, our past and our future. They may have particular implications for those who have been adopted, and who may have very little information about their genetic inheritance. This chapter will mainly explore potential implications, as research in this area is only just beginning.

Psychological identity

'Identity' – the question of 'who am I?' – is a complex notion. Like all our psychological characteristics, it is a function of social influences and biological make-up, both past and current influences, and past origins. The question 'who am I?' is often closely followed by 'where did I come from?' Again, this has social and biological components. Indeed, people are as interested in the social roles of their past family members as in their physical attributes.

There is a suggestion that the current discoveries of human genes are placing a greater emphasis on people's genetic, rather than their social, heritages. Writing in *Nature*, Maddox suggests that one consequence of the increasing press coverage of these genetic discoveries is a 'growing belief in a kind of genetic predestination'.[1] If this is the case, it may have a greater effect on adopted children than non-adopted children.

Children who are adopted face several losses: their birth family and its social environment, and access to their family history, and hence their cultural and genealogical heritage. The developing practice of more open adoption is likely to ameliorate some of these losses.

Research into adopted children's adaptation to these losses suggests that it is not until adolescence that such losses may cause problems.[2] Adolescence is a time in which identity is often questioned and potentially developed. As the adolescent becomes more independent and separate from family and home, so the need for an autonomous identity grows. The questions 'who am I?', and 'where am I going?' raise the questions 'who made me?', and 'where did I come from?' It is at such time that a lack of knowledge about the birth family and a loss of 'connectedness' to a genealogical line may become acutely felt.

In a study of 50 adopted adolescents, Stein and Hoopes found that all had an interest in general background information, and 16 were actively seeking more information about their birth parents.[3] An example of how this is expressed comes from a 17-year-old in the study:

I only want to see if I look like my natural parents . . . if I did then I'd want to see if I was like them in any other way. If it was good, I'd like it because then I'd hope to be like that when I got older. I'd also like to see if my interests matched theirs, to see if they were hereditary or environmental. I wonder how tall they were . . . I'd want to see their kids to see if they would look like I did.

There are two conflicting views on why adopted children want more information about their birth families. One is that such children are 'genealogically bewildered', experiencing confusion and uncertainty that undermines their security and mental health.[4] The lack of family background knowledge in the (adopted) adolescent has been said to prevent the development of a healthy genetic ego, which is then replaced by a 'hereditary ghost'.[5] Since the genetic ego is obscure, the adolescent has no way of knowing what might be passed on to the next generation. Curiosity about birth parents has also been seen as a sign of psychological stress or poor adoptive experience.[6] Such views, however, remain speculative, being based on clinical experience and interpretation, rather than on empirical studies of representative samples of adopted children.

The other view is that the desire for more information is a normal part of the process of separating from parents, which helps to create a social identity.

Haimes' study of 45 adopted individuals found that those who wanted to trace their birth parents were well-adjusted and were motivated by curiosity rather than crisis or pathology.[7] Their motivation was to discover their life-story in order to compile a complete and consistent biography for themselves. In one of the few controlled research studies using normative populations of adopted and non-adopted adolescents, Stein and Hoopes found that adopted adolescents did not show more problems of identity or adjustment.[8] One of their conclusions was that adoptive parents need to be made aware that their adolescent's interest in more general information about his or her origins is a normal and healthy manifestation of the process of identity consolidation.

Interest in our origins is seen by Haimes as a cultural, rather than an individual, phenomenon. As the science and technologies of genetics become more pervasive within our culture, it is likely that adopted people will become *more* rather than *less* interested in their genetic origins. One would predict the opposite from the 'genealogically bewilderment' view. As the adoption process is becoming more open and enabling the psychological needs of adopted people and their families to be more fully met, so one would predict that the desire for information about the birth family would be *less* frequent than in the past. This is an empirical question worthy of study.

Adolescence is a time of increasing awareness of the body and physical self-image. At such a time, physical differences between the adopted individual and his or her adoptive family may become more apparent and a curiosity about the physical appearance of the birth family may grow. There is some evidence that adolescents who are interested in searching for information about their birth family are those who perceive themselves as more different physically from their adoptive parents.[9]

Adolescents may also become more health conscious than previously. In Haimes' study of adolescents searching for information about their birth families,[10] 16 out of 50 adolescents expressed an interest in family history information, with health history heading the list. Biological information about the birth family can give clues about the timing and course of the adopted person's physical maturation, both during adolescence and over the life span. It can also give information about vulnerability to diseases that have a genetic link.

There is increasing emphasis on genetics as a contributor to health. In a series of interviews with a sample of the general population, heredity was seen as the major cause of health.[11] In another study heredity was seen as the third major cause of illness, after germs and life style.[12] People may now also have the impression that not merely their physical well-being but also their behaviour is determined by the genes they happen to have inherited.[13] For example, there have been recent well-publicised reports of possible genetic inheritance for the largely socially determined characteristics of homosexuality, aggression and shyness.

We know that genetic make-up can be a powerful contributor to one's image of oneself. For example, one study has found that those at risk for Huntington's disease, but found not to carry the gene, were likely to suffer from guilt and depression.[14] The authors argue that one reason for this is that an important part of their identity, their genetic identity, had been dramatically changed.

As awareness of the genetic contribution to our lives increases, so the effects of not knowing this contribution may increase. The issue of genetic disease and the ability to avoid such disease in one's future children is being given greater attention in health services and in the media. These factors may lead to an increased anxiety about not knowing about one's genetic history and an increased tendency to search for information about one's birth family. Providing people with information about their genetic make-up may affect how they think, feel and behave in relation to their health, their image of themselves and their decisions to have children.[15] If information about genetic make-up is a bigger issue for adopted children due to its relative absence and difficulties in searching, such effects may be greater for them than for those not adopted.

Some behaviours, as well as diseases, are being shown to be genetically related. For example, some authors have suggested that there is a link between criminality and alcohol abuse. These behaviours are frequent in the birth parents of children who have been adopted.[16] Increasing knowledge about genetics and the increasing public discussion may cause increasing worry amongst adopted people about these issues: if they think that their birth parents are in some way 'biologically inferior', their own self-esteem may be threatened. This is supported by a study that found that unfavourable reports about birth parents were associated with identity problems in adopted adolescents.[17] The latter took the reports to be proof of their biological parents' inferiority and, hence, their own genetic inferiority. This may be confounded by a perception in adopted people that their adoptive parents would have preferred children sharing their own genes, rather than those of other, unknown people.

It must be said that much of this is hypothetical; there have been few empirical studies comparing adopted with non-adopted adolescents in which these issues have been explored.

Information for adoptive parents

The new developments in genetics also have implications for adoptive parents. One question that is raised is whether adoptive parents should be given full information about the child's genetic history before adoption. This may be helpful for the parent and/or the child. The argument for full information is similar to that used in family therapy: acceptance of the known facts, however distasteful, is associated with improved family relationships. The argument against this is that it may be feeding into an over-emphasis on genetic, as opposed to social and psychological, aspects of the child and his or her environment.

In some countries, such as the USA, adopted children have no legal right to obtain information about their birth families. The uncertainties of childhood may therefore persist throughout life. In other countries, such as Britain, Finland, Israel and Sweden, adopted children may obtain what information exists about their birth family at the age of 17 or 18 years. The teenage years are often ones of instability and insecurity, especially concerning questions of identity. This raises the question of whether the ages of 17 or 18 are the most appropriate for such information to be made available, or whether there would be psychological advantages to children being brought up knowing that such information is available if they should wish to seek it. The weight of evidence indicates that adopted persons who inquire about their origins cope better when they are given the information, rather than being left to worry about the unknown.[18]

Predictive testing in children

Recent advances in molecular genetics have led to the ability to test individuals for an increasing range of genetic diseases and conditions that may not become apparent until later life. Tests fall broadly into two categories:

1. the prediction of disease risk for late onset single gene conditions, where gene penetrance is 100 per cent (eg. Huntington's disease, myotonic dystrophy, familial adenomatous polyposis, polycystic kidney disease); and

2. testing for risk factors for multifactorial and polygenic diseases eg. heart disease, diabetes, some cancers.

Although predictive testing is not routinely offered to children, some parents are approaching GPs and genetics clinics with requests for such testing. Little is currently known about the effects of predictive testing for the child and the family, either short-term emotional adjustment, or the long-term effects of coping with any subsequent illness. Given the frequent lack of information about the genetic history of adopted children, adoptive parents and the children themselves may be especially interested in the possibility of predictive testing. This may have direct consequences for the adoptive placement of children.

The more that can be known about genetic disease, the more aware individuals may become about what they do not know. This is especially true of adopted children, where family history may be absent or scant. Adopted children may lack both the knowledge of genetic disease or conditions in their birth family, and the possibility of tracing genes by family linkage or mutation analysis. They may therefore face a double dose of uncertainty: uncertainty as to whether any genetic problems exist in their family medical history *and* uncertainty as to whether they have inherited any problems that may exist or have existed. This uncertainty may lead to psychological problems where children feel unsure about their identity and experience greater stress. Adopted children have been found to be more vulnerable to these problems than average.[19]

Predictive genetic testing gives the possibility of resolving some of these uncertainties. As expressed by Schechter and Bertocci,[20] 'the capacity to anticipate the future serves in part as a survival mechanism; it fortifies the individual's sense of potential control over forthcoming events in life experience and, in so doing, maintains anxiety at manageable levels.'

The question of whether children should be offered testing has led to much debate which, at present, is mainly restricted to health professionals. As there have been few studies of children and families undergoing predictive testing, this debate is mainly informed by anecdotes rather than by empirical evidence. In addition to the views of health professionals, the views of parents and of children need to be considered. We need research on the psychological effects of testing on children and families at risk of late onset of disease *before* decisions are made about the availability of such testing. Some of the possible pros and cons of predictive testing in childhood that have been put forward are listed below.

Possible disadvantages
1. The child's self-esteem and long-term adjustment may be impaired.
2. The family's perception and treatment of the child may be adversely affected.
3. There may be discrimination in education and career choices.
4. Discrimination in financial security (life insurance/mortgage).

Possible advantages
1. There may be improved short-term and long-term psychological adjustment for the child.
2. Testing may relieve parental anxiety or uncertainty and avoids problems associated with "family secrets".
3. Allows child to take informed decisions from an early age, such as educational choices, and to plan practically for the future.

In order to establish the effects of predictive testing on the experience of adopted children, we need research in two key areas:
1. *Psychological effects:* What are the psychological effects upon adopted children of being found to be at high, or low, risk for a late onset disease? How does it affect their identity and self-esteem? Which effects are general, and which specific to the experience of being adopted?
2. *Family life:* How does predictive testing in a child affect relationships within their adoptive family, and their view of themselves within this family?

Pregnancy with little or no known family history

As young people approach reproductive age and consider their own future parenting, the questions of what kind of children they are likely to have, and whether those children will be healthy, are raised. Those who are adopted may have less information with which to answer or think about these questions, than those in contact with their birth families. When considering pregnancy or after having become pregnant, women who have been adopted may want more information about their family, including genetic, history. Thinking about one's own future parenting may also highlight the issue of why the adopted person's birth parents chose not to parent them: could the reasons be genetically related? Is there genetic disease within the family?

Pregnancy is an uncertain time for most women. One of the major concerns is that something may be wrong with the baby.[21] This uncertainty may be greater since the woman (who has been adopted) is likely to have less information on familial diseases or the obstetric history of her mother than a (non-adopted) pregnant woman. We do not have any empirical evidence about this. If it were shown to be the case that pregnant women (who were adopted) experienced greater anxiety because of their genetic uncertainty, there may be an argument for offering the widest range of genetic tests to them.

The increasing emphasis on genetic testing in antenatal care may be unhelpful in focusing attention away from other emotional issues that pregnant women may want to, or need to, address. For example, adopted people may undergo genetic testing to reduce uncertainty as a way of compensating for other areas in which they are unable to reduce their uncertainty. This may mean that they do not fully think through the implications of genetic testing or that they do not address the issue of what is causing the distress surrounding uncertainty. This distress may be exacerbated by giving birth, which may trigger feelings and worries in the mother of having been rejected by her birth mother. Because of the particular situation and needs of the adopted mother, it is important that genetic testing does not become a focus of diversion away from counselling about other emotional issues facing women at this stage of their life-cycle.

Conclusion

The theme running through this chapter is the host of psychological questions raised by the new genetics for the adoption process which are untouched by researchers' hands. Speculation is interesting and a crucial first step of the scientific process. If we are to gain knowledge about what *is* going on, rather than ideas about what *might* be going on, it is vital that research is done in this area. The main need, as always, is for well-designed and controlled studies that can answer particular questions, rather than case reports or retrospective, descriptive studies. Only in this way can the emotional and practical needs of adoptive families be sensitively and effectively addressed.

Acknowledgements

Both authors of this chapter are supported by a programme grant from the Wellcome Trust entitled: Psychological and Social Aspects of the New Genetics.

References

1 Maddox J, 'Has nature overwhelmed nurture?' *Nature*, 366:107, 1993.

2 Schechter M D, and Bertocci D, 'The Meaning of the Search', *The Psychology of Adoption*, (ed) Brodzinsky D M, and Schechter M D, Oxford University Press, 1990.

3 Stein L M, and Hoopes, J L, *Identity formation in the adopted adolescent*, Child Welfare League of America, USA, 1985.

4 Sants H J, 'Genealogical bewilderment in children with substitute parents', *British Journal of Medical Psychology*, 37:133-141, 1964.

5 Frisk M, 'Identity problems and confused conceptions of the genetic ego in adopted children during adolescence', *Acto Paedo Psychiatrica*, 31:6-12, 1964.

6 Triseliotis J, *In search of origins*, Routledge and Kegan Paul, 1973.

7 Haimes E, 'Now I know who I really am: Identity change and redefinitions of the self in adoption', Honess T, and Yardley K, (eds.) *Self and Identity*, Routledge and Kegan Paul, 1987.

8 See 3 above.

9 See 3 above.

10 See 7 above.

11 Herzlick C, *Health and Illness*, Academic Press, 1973.

12 Pill R, and Stott N, 'Concepts of illness causation and responsibility: Some preliminary data from a sample of working class mothers', In Currer C, Stacey M (eds), *Concepts of Health, Illness and Disease: A comparative approach,* Berg Publishers Ltd, 1986.

13 See 1 above.

14 Tibben A, Vegtor van den Vlis M, Niermeijer M F, et al, 'Testing for Huntington's Disease with support for all parties', *Lancet*, 335:553, 1990.

15 Marteau T M, 'Psychological implications of genetic screening. Birth Defects', *Original Article Series*, 28:185-190, 1992.

16 Bohman M, and Sigvardsson S, 'Outcome in Adoption: lessons from longitudinal studies', *The Psychology of Adoption*, (eds) Brodzinsky D M, and Schechter M D, Oxford University Press, 1990.

17 See 5 above.

18 See 2 above.

19 Brodzinsky D M, 'A stress and coping model of adoption adjustment', *The Psychology of Adoption*, (eds), Brodzinsky D M, and Schechter M D, Oxford University Press, 1990.

20 See 2 above.

21 Reid M, 'Consumer-oriented studies in relation to prenatal screening tests', *European Journal of Obstetrics, Gynecology, Reproduction and Biology*, 28: 79-92, 1988.

14 Genetic testing in children: the relevance for adoption

Dr Angus Clarke and Dr Heather Payne

Genetic testing for inherited disorders is of wide significance in adoption. The management of testing for genetic orders is a complex issue. This paper begins by distinguishing between the various tests – predictive, those that determine carrier status, diagnostic testing and genetic screening – and then goes on to examine those situations in which testing is appropriate and justified. Keeping the child's best interests at the forefront of their discussion, the authors consider the tensions between the dangers of labelling by testing and the value of knowledge.

It is with the advent of molecular genetic techniques that direct testing for faulty genes has widened the scope of predictive and carrier testing enormously. This raises new ethical dilemmas when such testing is requested for children who are currently healthy, and are unlikely to participate fully in the decision to be tested.

Concerns about the ethical implications of predictive testing in children were first raised in the context of Huntington's disease (HD), a dementing illness associated with chorea that usually presents in middle life.[1] These concerns led to a consensus that predictive testing for HD should not be performed.[2,3,4] These concerns were strengthened by the finding that only 10-15 per cent of at-risk adults came forward for predictive testing when it became available[5,6,7] and that test results can impose a significant psychosocial burden even when the results are favourable.[8,9]

The grounds for concern about predictive genetic testing for HD are essentially threefold.

1. The child's future autonomy as an adult will be lost if predictive testing has been performed in childhood. This is particularly worrying since so many adults choose not to be tested when they have the opportunity.

2. If a child is tested, the result will be given to the parents and may then be told to other relatives, neighbours, the child's school, the staff of

the local health centre etc . . . The confidentiality that an adult would be entitled to may be completely lost when the test is performed in childhood.

3. The parents' knowledge of their child's genetic status may distort the child's upbringing; expectations of the child's future career, intellect, relationships, procreation, etc, may all be affected, and any unfavourable expectations may become self-fulfilling prophecies long before the HD gene itself would have had any adverse effect at all.

Once these concerns had been raised in the context of HD, the question inevitably arose of whether HD was unique, or whether the same concerns might also apply to predictive testing for other disorders, or to testing children to identify unaffected carriers of recessive genetic disorders.[10] The ethical issues of autonomy and confidentiality will apply in principle to predictive testing for any adult-onset genetic disorder, and to any carrier status testing as well. As to the question of harm caused by such testing, there is scarcely any evidence upon which to base a judgement – even in the case of HD.

Population newborn screening (predictive testing) in Sweden for a condition that can present in infancy but which may also present in adult life – alpha-1-antitrypsin deficiency – was abandoned because of emotional trauma resulting from establishing the diagnosis in presymptomatic young infants.[11] This, however, may not be a good model for predictive testing in high-risk families for disorders that do not present usually until adult life because it was a population screening programme. Where carrier testing has been performed in childhood for many years (eg. with the cytogenetic identification of unaffected carriers of balanced chromosomal translocations) there have been no published studies of the psychosocial effects, so no information is available as to whether the testing process causes or prevents harm in practice.

At this point we should make it clear that there are genetic tests in childhood that it is clearly appropriate to perform, such as diagnostic investigations for a child who already has a clinical disorder that could be genetic in origin. Similarly, it may be appropriate to perform tests for a child who is at risk of a disease that would be likely to manifest clinically during childhood. Predictive testing may also be appropriate if a programme of health surveillance for complications of the disorder would be instituted on children identified as carrying the disease-associated allele, as with some family cancer syndromes: the child stands to benefit directly from surveillance for complications if he or she has the genetic condition in question, and to benefit from reassurance and the avoidance of unnecessary surveillance if not affected. These types of predictive testing for the direct benefit of the child, or where the condition would be likely to present in childhood in any case, we would regard as unproblematic; the rest of this chapter refers to predictive testing for late-onset disorders, or to carrier status tests, in neither of which situation does the child stand to benefit directly from the testing for some years, if at all.

Clinical Genetics Society Working Party Report on the Genetic Testing of Children

Because of the lack of any clear consensus approach to the issues raised by the genetic testing of children, the Clinical Genetics Society formed a Working Party to examine current professional attitudes and practices in this area and to encourage discussion of the issues. It was clear from the Report of this Working Party[12] that considerable numbers of children do have their carrier status determined for a variety of recessive disorders (even excluding neonatal screening for haemoglobinopathies), and that predictive tests for adult-onset disorders are also performed. However, there was no professional consensus, and indeed it was clear that there were substantial differences in attitude both within and between various professional groups.

These differences in attitude between groups were interesting. Genetic nurses/counsellors generally regarded predictive or carrier testing in childhood as undesirable, unless the child clearly stood to gain from it medically. Some clinical geneticists would perform tests on children at the request of their parents, but only selectively (for certain disorders only, not as a parental "right"). Paediatricians appeared more "liberal" in their approach, with most paediatricians expressing their willingness to perform genetic tests (predictive or carrier status) on children at the request of their parents. Many paediatricians even appeared willing to perform predictive tests on children for Huntington's disease.

These differences in response to the questionnaire between professional groups, we believe, are likely to reflect differences in experience with genetic testing, rather than deep differences in ethical values. Paediatricians have not generally had personally to confront the problems raised by predictive testing for HD in adults, while geneticists and genetic nurses will be much more familiar with such tests in practice. However, paediatricians' lack of experience with the problems of genetic testing could be important in the future if these tests become readily available through commercial channels with a financial interest in promoting such tests, and accessible without genetic counselling. At present, most health service molecular genetic diagnostic laboratories have close links with clinical geneticists, and many of the possibly inappropriate requests are vetted, and discussed with the referring clinician, before the tests are performed. This safeguard might well be lost if the laboratory services are separated from their associated clinical genetic services on grounds relating to the introduction of market forces into health service provision.

Adoption and genetic testing

The issues relating to genetic disease and genetic testing in the context of adoption are complex, and are considered in detail in other contributions to this collection. However, we will raise the question as to whether there are particular problems that might arise with the predictive or carrier testing of a child in the context of adoption, or whether there are particular considerations that might justify such testing of a child who is being considered for adoption. In this discussion, we draw very heavily upon the Report of the Clinical Genetics Society Working Party on the Genetic Testing of Children.[13]

It must be remembered that prospective adoptive parents may have a keen interest in the genetic status of a child that they are considering for adoption. Like most people (if given the choice) adopters will usually want healthy children, and the adoption agency is under an obligation to gather information about the child's circumstances, including the health of the child and of members of the family. All relevant available information is then given to prospective adopters so that they can make as informed a decision as possible when deciding whether to adopt a child. Good practice indicates that all available information should be passed on.

Tests of carrier status

There will usually be no particular justification for testing the child any earlier than would be the case with a child still in the birth family. Adoptive parents have the same legitimate interests in the health of their children and grandchildren as do biological parents. Two difficulties may arise from carrier testing a child in any family.

First, the family may be given information of possible relevance to the child's future reproductive plans, but may fail to remember this, or to understand its significance, or to pass it on to the child at an appropriate age. Secondly, the parents may focus on the possible carrier status of their child and accord it more emotional significance than is warranted.

In these situations, the lack of familiarity of an adoptive family with the condition in question may complicate the task of discussing the issues with the growing child, leading to over- or under-emphasis on the possibility of "genetic risk". Difficulties of communication may also arise when a genetic disease in the birth family comes to light after the adopted child has been settled in the new family. Similar problems of communication may arise in reverse if the adopted child develops a genetic disease after settling in the adoptive family. In either case, communication between the two families – through the adoption agency – may simply fail to occur by oversight.

Openness between adoptive parents and child, and the maintenance of links between the adoption agency and both the adoptive and the birth families, may help to minimise these problems. The questions of principle relating to carrier testing in childhood are little different in the context of adoption from the issues encountered in other families, even if the pathways of communication are more vulnerable to rupture. They do not amount to a reason for ensuring that the tests are carried out pre-placement.

The child with special needs

Adopters vary greatly in what they are prepared to consider in a child. For example, some will consider any health background except mental illness (most often specifically schizophrenia), while others could not accept a child with a family history of epilepsy. Some adopters will consider a child where paternity is unknown, but will exclude from consideration a child with a background of mental illness or incest.

Because of changes in the sorts of children available for adoption, prospective adopters who can accept a child with special needs are increasingly in demand. A corresponding shift in the expectations of adoptive applicants, however, has generally been slower to happen. The child who may develop a serious condition in the future (eg. schizophrenia), or who may develop a serious complication of a condition they already have (eg. neurofibromatosis), usually needs to be considered in the same category as a child who actually has special needs, and both situations call for particular qualities on the part of prospective adopters.

Predictive testing
For adult-onset conditions where predictive genetic testing is available, and where the adoptive child is at risk, the question arises as to whether or not the fact of the child's adoption (prospective or established) is a justification for carrying out a predictive test which might not otherwise be performed until the adopted child became an adult and chose to undergo testing. It could be maintained that appropriate carers may more easily be found for the child if genetic tests were performed. This might be so even if the results were unfavourable, as carers may find uncertainty more difficult to cope with than bad news, and the balance of benefits may then be very difficult to determine.

Predictive tests for Huntington's disease have been requested by adoption agencies on the assumption that a test result would facilitate an appropriate placement for the child.[14,15] But would it really help – particularly if the child is shown to have the HD gene? And would such testing leave the child vulnerable to future discrimination in the fields of life and health insurance[16] and employment?[17] And could testing lead to altered expectations of the child's abilities, future relationships, etc, on the part of the adoptive parents, as may happen in families where the biological parents and children are together?

Specific arguments against predictive testing in the context of adoption include the following:

(i)   that the diagnosis will label the child and affect the (already difficult) process of identity development;

(ii) that it does not contribute to meeting the need of the child for acceptance as he/she currently is; and

(iii) that it may cause more problems by identifying non-paternity which had not previously been suspected.

The arguments will have to be weighed in each case, but their force will not differ greatly from the standard case of a child in the original birth family, *unless* it proves difficult to find suitable prospective adoptive parents for a child at risk of a late-onset genetic disorder *because of the uncertainty surrounding the child's possible genetic status.* Then, decisions about the long-term plans for the child (including the decision to put the child forward for adoption, and the choice of carer), and the decision about genetic testing, may need to be reconsidered. In practice, this situation will arise only infrequently, but will call for a careful weighing of the child's overall best interests when it does so.

In general, it would seem best, wherever possible, to find adopters who can accept the child as a whole, and subsequently participate in any testing that is appropriate for the child as a confirmed member of their family.

Finally, it should be noted that the status of a child at risk of developing a genetic disorder (even in adult life) has some parallels with the status of a child with special needs. These include financial implications for the local authority, as a child who is at "high risk of developing a medical condition", known at the time of placement, may require an adoption allowance, payable until the age of 18.[18]

Genetic screening before placement for adoption

The important distinction between genetic diagnostic testing and genetic screening must be made clear at this point. Diagnostic testing of individuals for a disease that is known to run in their family entails testing persons who are at high risk of this disease. On the other hand, screening individuals for a disease entails testing whole populations of people who are, individually, at low risk. This is very different from diagnostic testing because the mass nature of the test may lead to its being prone to errors (having significant false negative and false positive rates), and because the level of understanding of the screening test by those tested may be inadequate unless those offering the test devote much energy to ensuring that all those tested understand the implications of the possible test results before the test is performed (and give their informed consent to the test).

In addition to the possibility of performing genetic tests for diseases known, or thought, to be present in the biological family of the child being considered for adoption, there will soon arise the question of whether *any* child being considered for adoption should have genetic tests performed to screen for a battery of genetic conditions or susceptibilities. Where there is no professional consensus that the child's health care will be improved by the results of this testing (so that *all* children are recommended to have tests performed only in their own interests), we would suggest that such tests could be contrary to the best interests of the child. The tested child may be placed at greater risk of stigmatisation and discrimination within an adoptive family, or may not be adopted at all, or may find that he or she is liable to institutional discrimination in the future (in life or health insurance, in employment, in education, etc). We do not believe that adoptive children should be singled out for such genetic tests when the potential for damage from distorted family relationships is so great for them in any case.

One condition for which mass screening is already technically possible, and for which every child referred for adoption could easily be screened, is Fragile X mental retardation (FRAXA), the commonest familial form of mental disability. Would such a screening programme be acceptable? Unless such testing fulfills the established criteria for a screening programme, the answer must surely be in the negative.

There are two particular problems with this proposal, which is already under serious discussion by adoption authorities in the UK.[19] First, the adoptive parents may come to possess genetic information about the biological parents, which the biological parents do not possess. In some circumstances this may be unavoidable, but it is undesirable to establish this situation as routine.

Second, the knowledge gained may well not be helpful to anyone, and least of all to the child. When there is a family history of learning difficulties in the biological family, this may be considered in the planning of investigations if the child presents with developmental delay or learning difficulties. But the knowledge that the adoptive child has an expansion of the Fragile-X-associated triplet repeat at the FMR-1 gene may be unhelpful when the child has shown no evidence of being clinically affected. Particularly with a girl, but even with boys, the child's level of ability is not accurately predicted by the molecular genetic results. It may be difficult for parents, teachers, social workers or others to forget that a child has an expansion at the FRAXA site, and this could lead to unfavourable expectations of the child's intellectual abilities; such unfavourable expectations can certainly become self-fulfilling prophecies.

For an infant, it may well be best for the child if his or her carers and teachers do not treat him as "genetically flawed" from the very outset. If the child subsequently shows signs of educational difficulties then the diagnosis of FRAXA may become established at that stage, but that will be more appropriate and the damage from prejudicing expectations will be less likely to arise because the child's level of abilities will already be apparent. While there may be some benefit to an affected child if the cause of their acknowledged learning impairment is recognised (although this is not in any sense established, it is an item of faith among some professionals), there are no grounds for thinking that a child will benefit from the diagnosis of FRAXA being established even before any grounds for concern have been identified. Indeed, the diagnostic labelling of children who clearly already have severe intellectual and neurological impairments as part of a syndrome of developmental delay and congenital anomalies can result in great distress within the family if the extent of the child's manifest problems has not already been accepted at the emotional level. The screening and labelling of apparently "normal" infants and children as being affected by FRAXA should be approached with great caution if comparable (not identical) difficulties are to be avoided.

Many children with FRAXA mutations show very minor cognitive difficulties, and present with behavioural rather than intellectual problems; for these children, being labelled as cases of Fragile X mental retardation before any learning disabilities have appeared could exacerbate their problems. There has certainly been no evidence that parental and professional knowledge of their Fragile X status has been of any value to such children, and there are good grounds for fearing the opposite. It would be unwise to initiate an uncontrolled test of this hypothesis in a cohort of adoptive children, with no suggestive family history of Fragile X, without solid grounds for doing so. However, there is a tension between the dangers of 'labelling' by testing and the value of 'knowing' particularly in the case of female carriers.

Conclusion

Genetic testing for inherited disorders has a wide range of significance in adoption because of the multiplicity of potentially conflicting interests that exist among the members of the adoption triangle (adopted person, birth family, adoptive family) and the adoption agency. When inherited disorders arise in the context of adoption placement decisions, they may be highly significant and have an important bearing on the outcome of an adoption.

The management of testing for genetic disorders in adoption should commence with determining the attitudes and expectations of adopters with regard to present or future disability. The issues of predictive and carrier testing in adoption are much the same as for any other individual at genetic risk, but with the additional consideration of the effect of the decision (and, if a test is performed, the possible test results) on the child's placement. It should not be assumed that genetic testing (predictive or carrier) will be required before a suitable placement can be achieved. In each case, we would advise discussion between the medical adviser to the adoption agency and a clinical geneticist. The important factors other than the possible laboratory test results need to be identified for future attention before any test is performed. The legal situation regarding consent to testing in the adoption process has not been clarified judicially.

Adoption agencies do have a legitimate interest in the genetic status of prospective adoptive children, in so far as the results of any genetic testing may influence the likelihood of a child being accepted by suitable adoptive parents. However, it may be better for a child to be adopted by parents whose willingness to adopt is not dependent upon the performance or the results of predictive or carrier genetic tests. This consideration applies to genetic screening for Fragile X mental retardation as well as to family-specific genetic diagnostic testing.

Acknowledgements

We would like to acknowledge first our debt to our colleagues on the Clinical Genetics Society Working Party on the Genetic Testing of Children, who have contributed enormously to the development of the ideas in this chapter. Furthermore, we are grateful to the Clinical Genetics Society for permission to quote so extensively from the Working Party's Report.

We are also grateful to all our other colleagues who have discussed these issues with us, and to financial support from the Marie Stopes Research Fund (administered by the Galton Institute), which made possible the attitude survey on which the Working Party Report is based.

References

1 Craufurd D, Harris R, 'Ethics of predictive testing for Huntington's chorea: the need for more information', *British Medical Journal*, 293:249-251, 1986.

2 World Federation of Neurology, Research Committee Research Group Ethical issues policy statement on Huntington's disease molecular genetics predictive test, *Journal of Neurological Science*, 94:327-332, 1989, *Journal of Medical Genetics*, 27:34-38, 1990.

3 See 2 above.

4 Bloch M, Hayden M R, 'Opinion: Predictive testing for Huntington disease in childhood: challenges and implications', *American Journal of Human Genetics*, 46:1-4, 1990, USA.

5 Craufurd D, Dodge A, Kerzin-Storrar L, Harris R, 'Uptake of presymptomatic testing for Huntington's disease', *Lancet*, ii:603-5, 1989.

6 Tyler A, Morris M, Lazarou L, Meredith L, Myring J, Harper P S, 'Presymptomatic testing for Huntington's Disease in Wales 1987-1990', *British Journal of Psychiatry,* 161:481-489, 1992.

7 Bloch M, Adam S, Wiggins S, Huggins M, Hayden M R, 'Predictive testing for Huntington disease in Canada: The experience of those receiving an increased risk', *American Journal of Medical Genetics*, 42:499-507, 1992, USA.

8 Huggins M, Bloch M, Wiggins S, Adam S, Suchowersky O, Trew M, Klimek M L, Greenberg C R, Eleff M, Thompson L P, Knight J, MacLeod P, Girard

K, Theilmann J, Hedrick A, Hayden M R, 'Predictive testing for Huntington Disease in Canada: Adverse effects and unexpected results in those receiving a decreased risk', *American Journal of Medical Genetics*, 42:508-515, 1992, USA.

9 Tibben A, Vegter-van der Vlis M, Skraastad M I, et al, 'DNA testing for Huntington's disease in The Netherlands: a retrospective study on psychosocial effects', *American Journal of Medical Genetics,* 44:94-99, 1992, USA.

10 Harper PS, Clarke A, 'Should we test children for "adult" genetic diseases?', *Lancet*, 335:1205-6, 1990.

11 Thelin T, McNeil T F, Aspegren-Jansson E, and Sveger T, 'Psychological consequences of neonatal screening for alpha-1-antitrypsin deficiency' *Acta Paediatr Scand* 74:787-793, 1985.

12 Working Party of the Clinical Genetics Society (chair, A Clarke), *Report on the Genetic Testing of Children*, Clinical Genetics Society, 1994, and *Journal of Medical Genetics*, 31:785-797, 1994.

13 See 12 above.

14 Morris M, Tyler A and Harper P S, 'Adoption and genetic prediction for Huntington's disease', *Lancet*, ii:1069-70, 1988.

15 Morris M, Tyler A, Lazarou L, Meredith L, Harper P S, 'Problems in genetic predication for Huntington's disease', *Lancet*, ii:601-3, 1989.

16 Harper P S, 'Insurance and genetic testing', *Lancet*, 341:224-227, 1993.

17 Billings P R, Kohn M A, de Cuevas M, Beckwith J, Alper J S, Natowicz M R, 'Discrimination as a consequence of genetic testing', *American Journal of Human Genetics*, 30:476-482, 1992.

18 Department of Health, *Children Act 1989 Regulations and Guidance Volume 9: 'Adoption Issues'*. Chapter 2, paragraph 2.31 (page 9), HMSO, 1991.

19 Turnpenny P D, Simpson S A, McWhinnie A M, 'Adoption, genetic disease, and DNA', *Archives of Diseases in Childhood*, 69:411-413, 1993.

15 Issues of confidentiality, disclosure and non-disclosure: medical perspectives

Professor J A Raeburn

How does the social worker or medical adviser know whether, and which, genetic information is important? Who needs to have the information? To whom does the genetic information belong? This chapter considers these and other questions, and discusses the ensuing issues of confidentiality, disclosure and non-disclosure. Illustrated with case studies, the paper then recommends some rules of disclosure.

Before considering the details of those situations in which confidentiality issues are of greatest importance, or giving guidelines about disclosure (when this is needed), it is useful to provide two "mission statements" about the relevant genetic information which should be sought and made available in connection with adoption. (Both of these were developed by the author.)

Genetic enquiries and investigations seek to identify important information about the genetic health of the adopted person or of his/her future children, so that this can be used for the individual's own good, without unnecessary infringement of the principle of confidentiality.

The central ethical issue is that adopted children should be accepted and nurtured in their new family with the same rights and privileges as any other family member.

The right to know

How does the social worker or medical adviser know whether information is important? Whose responsibility is it to obtain the family information? Who wants to have the information? Who needs the information?

Table 1 indicates those who would usually wish (and who have a right to) information about the adopted person's genetic background. The family information needed will depend on the genetic condition(s) which have been reported, on the findings of the clinical examination by the adopted person's doctor, and on factors relating to the suspected conditions such as the age of onset (especially whether this occurs in childhood or in adult life) and whether there are likely to be carriers of the condition who are completely healthy.

Table 1

Who needs to have genetic information about the adopted person?

The adoptive parents
The adopted person's family doctor
The adoption agency
The adopted person

How much information?

Adoptive parents should not expect to receive more information about the adopted child than birth parents would have about their own child. If this rule is followed, the adopted child is not subjected to more invasive family or genetic investigations than other children. The right of the adopted child to be treated in the same way as children growing up in their natural family may sometimes be challenged; if so, the reasons for more invasive investigation, including prying into the family history, must always be specified.

Individuals identified in Table 1 may have many reasons for wishing to know the genetic facts about the adopted child. It is obvious that the adoptive parents need knowledge, often before they decide about the adoption. Similarly, the adoption agency, acting as an intermediary between prospective and birth parents, needs to have relevant information, as does the family doctor. But the most compelling right to information is that of the adopted person; the other people in Table 1 hold this information 'in trust'.

An understandable concern with both the adoptive parents and the agency is that no stone is left unturned to identify possible health problems in the child who is being adopted. This may lead to the performance of genetic screening tests which would not be considered in the children born within the family. However, the anxieties of adoptive parents must not lead to pressures to investigate the child to excess. Whilst the guideline that "no tests are carried out that would not have been considered on a natural child" should be the central principle, the very nature of the adoption process will mean that agencies and prospective parents are attentive to the future problems that may arise.

Transferring responsibility

At what stage does responsibility for an adopted child's genetic history get transferred to the adoptive parents? Since this information belongs to the adopted child, the adoptive parents should appreciate their responsibility to pass it on, at an appropriate time and with appropriate professional support. The process of adoption should enhance this commitment to pass on genetic knowledge.

Since without relevant genetic information the adopted child's doctor cannot play a full part in the patient's medical care, he or she should also be fully informed. It seems appropriate that the GP is given full information as soon as the adoption has taken place, possibly by means of a letter from the geneticist.

Is anything secret?

Seen from a geneticist's viewpoint families may either be secretive or very open. Candour and openness is usually in the best interests of any child whether adopted or not. Can adoption procedures be performed in a manner which encourages frankness whilst recognising those facts which are personal and confidential?

Genetic information and how to handle it

The next part of this chapter focuses on the type of genetic information that may need to be made available to adoptive parents, along with some rules to help the adoption team to tackle the most likely scenarios. In the author's view, genetic information should not be sought too conscientiously, especially about diseases that may only occur in adult life. A fine line needs to be drawn between situations which merit disclosure and those which do not.

For example, adoptive parents need information about a risk of Huntington's disease even though this very rarely causes symptoms in childhood. The reason is that the interests of the at risk child may be best served by gradual disclosure towards adolescence. In adult life the adopted person can then choose whether or not to have predictive tests.

Case study 1

Baby A was aged four months when prospective adoptive parents began to consider his adoption. He was clinically well, as was his 24-year-old mother. She did not wish to declare who the father of her baby was but emphasised that she and the father were not related. This was important because her own parents were first cousins, and consanguineous marriages were the custom in the family. Her brother had an undiagnosed neurological condition which was probably autosomal recessive in inheritance. His symptoms began at age five and were progressive. The risk of neurological disease in baby A would be significantly increased if the father was related to baby A's mother and very low if not. The prospective adoptive parents asked if DNA based tests could be carried out on baby A and his mother to exclude a first cousin relationship.

This was not possible for many reasons including ethical grounds. Firstly, it would subject baby A to an unnecessary investigation. Secondly, the absence of the father meant that interpretation would inevitably be difficult and inaccurate as regards the identification of consanguinity. Thirdly, the mother did not agree to be tested.

The prospective adopters withdrew their application to adopt baby A; they could not come to terms with uncertainty about a possible genetic disease and the fact that it would be several years before they could be fully reassured.

Comment

Since many people find it difficult to deal with uncertainty, this aspect should be tackled directly and discussed in depth during pre-adoption counselling.

Case study 2

An adopted boy, aged 11, was happily integrated into a healthy family with two children of their own. Social workers then learned that the boy's birth father had died aged 40 with Huntington's disease, having fathered four other children, all of whom were also adopted. They informed the family GP who raised the matter with the adoptive parents, and referred the family to a genetic service. The adoptive parents were extremely anxious to learn of the diagnosis. They promised to arrange that the boy would be offered genetic counselling when he was older and that they would initiate disclosure. They suggested that a blood test should be taken (giving the boy only an excuse) in order to identify the presence or absence of the HD gene; they reasoned that if the result was negative, the boy need not be told.

The years have passed; for the boy school has led on to University and to medical training. The adoptive parents have not been able to bring up the subject themselves or to involve the genetic counselling team. The problem that looms is that their adopted son is now seeking his birth family and may well meet his siblings, two of whom *have* been informed of their father's diagnosis. When he discovers the situation he is likely to be very concerned and possibly angry.

Comment
There never is a 'right time' to disclose bad news. Might it have been easier for the adoptive parents if such issues were discussed (in theory) prior to adoption? A 'contract' about the disclosure of relevant new information which became available could have been agreed. It is always easier to address this type of issue earlier; any hesitancy can be managed by pointing out the consequences of not giving the information.

Rules of disclosure
With these examples in mind there now follows a group of simple rules to aid the approach to disclosure – or when relevant, non-disclosure – of genetic information.
1. The genetic information belongs to the adopted person and ideally this should be disclosed at the same age that natural children born within the family would have been told. In cases where the adopted person will not see their birth parents (and thus would have no opportunity to recognise ill-health and to ask leading questions) some brief reports about the parents and of possible illnesses may need to be given.

2. Questions about "my real parents" should be answered as directly as possible with the early involvement of professional genetic counselling help.

3. The genetic issues (eg. discussing the exact genetic risks with the adoptive parents) must be carried out with the support and knowledge of clinical geneticists, who would usually provide genetic counselling to the adopted person and the adoptive parents.

4. Some genetic diseases may be of no significance to the adopted person (eg. haemophilia in the biological father of a normal boy) and therefore no discussion with adoptive parents should occur without genetic advice.

5. No action should be taken to remove an adopted person's control over his/her life, for example, by destroying family records.

It is interesting that the Children Act 1989 makes clear the responsibilities of parents and other carers. It does not mention the need to empower the child to make his or her own decisions as he/she grows older.

The future

Many of the issues discussed above have received little attention and are not adequately researched. Experience should be documented and reported anonymously, including follow-up information about adopted people who have been informed of their family histories in different ways and at different ages.

It is important to seek genetic advice early. The first time that adoptive parents hear of a genetic problem will be the occasion that they remember most. It is essential that precise and accurate information is available at that time. An inaccurate description of a complex problem, by someone who is unaware of the genetic circumstances, may blight the opportunity to adopt or may store up intractable problems for all concerned.

16 Confidentiality, disclosure and non-disclosure of genetic information: legal perspectives

Alexandra Plumtree

What does confidentiality involve when applied to medical information? And is legal confidentiality different? This contribution explores these concepts and their application, with a special focus on genetic information and the adoption process.

'Confidentiality' when applied to information means that the information has been given with trust, and is not expected to be passed on without the consent of the person who has confided it. Confidentiality and the protection thereof are particularly important in the field of medicine, and medical information is protected. This protection means that, with certain exceptions, disclosure of information given to a doctor can lead to proceedings against that doctor for breach of confidence and resulting damages. There may be disciplinary procedures, and a striking off the roll of medical practitioners. There is also protection under the Data Protection Act 1984. The medical profession has developed wide ranging ethics and rules governing the question of confidentiality, and a doctor will generally be held to be in breach of confidence if he or she has broken these rules, even if there has been no actual law broken. It is on this basis that proceedings against a doctor for breach of confidence, etc. could arise.

Legal 'confidentiality' is a slightly different concept, in that a doctor can be ordered to disclose information by a court, notwithstanding the confidential relationship between doctor and patient. Such disclosure will only be ordered in exceptional circumstances, but a doctor does not have the same ultimate full protection as a solicitor in dealing with clients, and the doctor may therefore be ordered to disclose information in court proceedings, which information he or she would otherwise regard, quite properly, as confidential.

Basically, therefore, if a doctor holds confidential information on a patient, this should not be passed on to anyone else without the consent of the patient. There are, however, situations where such a breach will not attract retribution, as, for example, 'public interest'. Certain contagious diseases must be notified to the Public Health Authorities, so that protective steps may be taken. Similarly, protection of the vulnerable is a situation where breach of confidentiality is acceptable. Where a child is brought to a doctor with apparent non-accidental injuries, the doctor must take appropriate steps, involving disclosure of otherwise confidential information, so that a proper investigation may be made, with a view to protecting the child. The child's right to and need for protection override confidentiality in that sort of situation.

In most medical circumstances, an individual's medical information is of no direct relevance to anyone else, however much others may be interested in or concerned about it. The actual state of health of the patient does not in itself directly affect the health of the interested party or parties. This is not necessarily so with respect to genetic disease, because of the very nature of genetic information. Wide ranging, far reaching information may be available about a patient's genetic profile, which information in turn can have direct consequences for birth relatives. Keeping such information confidential may prevent the early diagnosis of serious illness in other relatives, reducing the chances of a cure and/or increasing the likelihood of an earlier death. Surely, it could be argued, the disclosure of the patient's information, even without his or her permission or consent, is desirable in order to prevent or reduce potential suffering in relatives at risk.

As a result of all this, the questions of breaching confidence and disclosing information, and if so to whom, are becoming increasingly difficult problems for medical geneticists to resolve. It has been said that society as a whole does not call upon strict rules or legislation about topics which are not yet seriously exercising the public mind[1] and many of the questions which arise as a result of the development of genetics, whether in law or elsewhere, have so far fallen into this category. There is an increasing awareness of the many problems, but despite growing concern and discussion over the last few years, there are no legislative provisions, and there are no Department of Health, Scottish Office, or

British Medical Association (BMA) guidelines. The law is not at all developed, and is a long way behind the very many scientific and medical developments. A practitioner, faced with a question of ethics arising from a genetics problem, is forced simply to consider the individual best course of action in that case. Doctors, if in doubt about whether to breach confidentiality or not, need to consider, discuss with colleagues, and possibly consult with the Medical Defence Union or equivalent. There may be cases where the general principle of confidentiality has to be abandoned.

For example, if a doctor is dealing with a family in which there is a history of genetic disease, what happens if one of the children of the family (the mother having died of the disease) discloses that another sibling is not actually the father's child? The sibling in question is not aware of this, and full predictive testing may not be possible given the unavailability of the real father's blood for screening purposes. If the only way to proceed is to breach the first sibling's disclosure of 'confidential' information by telling the second sibling, then notwithstanding the first sibling's wishes, it may well be argued that the second sibling's long-term interests outweigh the breaching of confidence, even given the general distress to everyone concerned. If the second sibling wishes predictive testing and it turns out to be impossible to achieve this without the birth father's markers, then the confidential information may have to be disclosed in order to investigate further and obtain these markers, and to explain the position to the second sibling.

There are innumerable practical and legal problems which arise given the ever increasing range of genetic information which can be obtained from screening, the different types of illness which may be diagnosed by screening, and the general fast pace of development. These problems arise in many areas, such as insurance, employment or, as in the present case, adoption. Should insurance companies be entitled to request screening for potential risks? Should employers have such a right? If so, in what circumstances?

Adoption: a special case
Adoption is an area, obviously, where these issues arise: Who can be tested? Who should be tested? Whose blood should be obtained for

screening purposes later? Should information about a child's genetic profile be disclosed to a child, and if so at what stage, and to what extent? Who owns the information? Who should disclose it and how?

These are problems which arise throughout the field of medical genetics, and the difficulty about adoption is that it complicates even further the obtaining of information: genetic profiles from birth parents; the tracing of birth families; and the tracing of adoptive children and their families following on information received, possibly many years afterwards, about the birth family themselves. In other words, the break that occurs in adoption between a birth family and the child, which break is often complete, means that the obtaining of information from either side for the other side is made even more difficult than with a family where there has been no such dramatic break. These problems are greatly increased by adoption, as are the problems of confidentiality and disclosure. Who owns the information? To whom should it be disclosed?

As indicated, the law is really of very little help in this area. The individual practitioner needs to appreciate this, and to realise that each case has to be looked at on its own basis, and proceeded with following advice and consultation. The Nuffield Council on Bio-ethics produced in December 1993 a Report entitled *Genetic Screening: Ethical issues*.[2] In it, the Council recommends that health professionals should seek to persuade individuals, if persuasion is necessary, to allow disclosure of relevant genetic information to other family members, and that there should be guidelines. It also considers that the accepted standards of confidentiality of medical information should be followed as far as possible, but that there would be exceptional circumstances where confidentiality might have to be overridden. It is not possible to say how a court would view this Report in any case before it, as it is only a Report and in no way binding. But it is to be hoped that a court would consider it as representing a fair starting point for deciding the issues.

So far as disclosure to the child of information regarding his/her genetic condition is concerned, an adopted child should be treated as any other child, so that if disclosure is appropriate, at a given age, and with proper counselling, this should be worked towards. The fact of adoption should not be allowed to stand in the way of such disclosure, and adopting/adoptive parents must be strongly encouraged to ensure proper disclosure of such information, and not to hide behind the adoption. At some point, these parents should be disclosing the fact that the child is adopted (if not already known), and just as this should be done delicately at the appropriate age, so proper disclosure of genetic and other medical information can be made to the child.

It is to be hoped that, at the very least, clear and helpful Guidelines are produced soon. The House of Commons Committee on Science and Technology is working on "Human Genetics" and expects to report in May or June 1995. This may lead to the issuing of such Guidelines in due course. Developing practice and law in this area needs to be done carefully and sensitively, and the passing of legislation as such will not necessarily assist, as that can often be the approach of taking a sledge-hammer to crack a nut. Preferably there will be well considered developments before some difficult crisis case produces an instant knee-jerk and inappropriate reaction from society.

References

1   Mason T K, and McCall Smith R A, *Law and Medical Ethics*, 4th edn, Butterworths, 1994.

2   *Genetic Screening: Ethical issues*, Nuffield Council on Bioethics, London, December 1993.

Postscript
Gene gazing: evolution or revolution in child care?

Donal Giltinan

Works of science, unlike works of literature and philosophy, do not generally endure. They act, rather, as milestones and signposts marking the long and sometimes circuitous route in our search for knowledge. This compendium of contributions on genetics in adoption and fostering is a marker anchoring our knowledge and our beliefs about the contribution that our understanding of genetics can make to adoption and fostering at the close of the 20th century. In our understanding and interpretation of genetics we need broad and open minds. In common with other scientific disciplines, genetics is largely inductive, made up of laws based on theories that flow from observation, classification and causal analysis. Some of these theories may in time be replaced by new theories flowing from new observations, or new interpretations of old observations by way of deduction, whereby the new theory provides the paradigm shift which replaces a previously held belief and rapidly moves our knowledge of genetics to new levels.

In 1859, John Murray published Darwin's theory of evolution by natural selection, *The Origin of Species*. It caused a great sensation, not because what it said was entirely new, but because it seemed to challenge firmly held beliefs about the need for a direct link between God and humanity. There is a story that the response among many of the clergy at that time was "let us hope it is not true: but if it is that it does not become generally known"! There were branches of the established church that were able to accept the validity of Darwin's theory and accommodate evolution within a theology of the cosmos. Natural selection might have been ordained by God as one of the means whereby humankind aspires to greater goodness and social development. However, the theory of evolution is itself likely to 'evolve', and may possibly be replaced by a new framework in due course, just as many earlier concepts in genetics have been radically revised.

The development of our knowledge in genetics presents child care workers in all disciplines with similar challenges to those presented by the evolutionists. Each new life comes into our world carrying a sealed envelope marked "personal and confidential". The challenges are two-fold and sequential. First, who has the right to open that envelope? Parents or guardians may wish to "read" this confidential information and may request help through predictive genetic testing to do so. This issue is dealt with by several of the contributors and they concur that predictive testing of children is appropriate only in circumstances where the onset of a particular condition occurs in childhood and there are useful interventions which can be offered. However, they also state that genetic testing of young children for an adult onset disease should not generally be undertaken, particularly if no preventive intervention can be offered. This reflects the recommendations of the working party report on the genetic testing of children which reported in March 1994.

The second challenge is that the dictionary explaining and translating the words in the envelope has only begun to be written and each day a few new words are translated, explained and added to this human lexicon. Geneticists can begin to string together several sentences from these words which will give us vital information about our potential for growth or our failure to thrive, and our capacity to inherit and recreate the salient features of our progenitors.

The secrets in our genes are only beginning to unfold and each new discovery casts further light, or sometimes doubt, on previously held beliefs. The clues to the secrets are hidden by time and space and generations and, as Morrison points out in Chapter 2, the genealogical discontinuity caused by adoption makes the search for clues extremely difficult.

It is perfectly reasonable for adoptive parents to wish to know as much background information as possible about the child they wish to adopt. Many experts in the field of adoption remind us of the genealogical bewilderment experienced by adopted people who know very little about their background, particularly when it is being probed by specialists who are seeking for clues about physical or psychological symptoms they may be displaying. Some adoption specialists would state that we should give adoptive parents "as much information as possible" about their child's background.

There is an emerging anomaly in our approach to the gathering of data about the health of children placed for adoption. Grant (Chapter 3) reminds us of the statutory duty to provide adoptive parents and foster carers with information about the child's health and background. Adoption practice might evolve by recommending agencies to develop close liaison with genetic centres, and by developing medical forms which reinforce the importance of family history. There needs to be further debate among child care workers, whether in the medical, social work or non-professional field, about the extent to which it is helpful to probe our genealogical past for clues about our future. That debate is underway and is being informed by longitudinal studies, such as the Colorado Adoption Project referred to by Turnpenny (Chapter 5). We need to know an awful lot more about what knowledge is useful and valuable and enhances the lives of people who are at the core of adoption and fostering before we can make unequivocal pronouncements about the application of genetic testing; in any event, to whom does the information belong?

All the behavioural sciences, and particularly social work, have prevaricated about the balance between nature and nurture in influencing human behaviour. Adoption has provided, perhaps, the most information rich source for testing out the myriad of hypotheses about this balance. More and more light is being cast on the balance of these influences as our genes reluctantly give up their secrets. Information for its own sake is not necessarily helpful and generalisations need to be grounded in real individual experiences. The rapidity of scientific advance needs to be tempered with questions about dignity and the enhancement of the human condition.

This collection of linked essays is an attempt by people in the fields of medicine, genetics, psychology, law, and social work, with a common interest in adoption and fostering, to come to grips with the responsible use of information about other people. Our knowledge about the behaviour of genes is still at a very early stage and, although growing in quantum leaps, there is little that can be definitively written about the subject. It is the shared hope of the contributors that readers will have found this book an information-rich source of material that will enhance the lives of both workers and families who are involved in adoption and fostering.

Glossary

Acrylamide (gel) The basic unit (monomer) of a resin which, when cross linked with other units, forms a 'polyacrylamide' gel used as the medium for separation of *DNA* fragments by *electrophoresis*.

Adenovirus Viruses are tiny infectious organisms which reproduce inside host *cells* and contain either *DNA* or *RNA* as their *genome*. Adenoviruses contain *DNA* and frequently cause the common cold.

Aetiology The origin or causation (of a disease).

Agarose (gel) Agarose is a starch-like chemical compound (polysaccharide) which forms an inert gelatinous matrix (gel) when dissolved in hot water and allowed to cool. The gel is used as the medium through which *DNA* fragments of different sizes are separated by *electrophoresis*.

Allele One member of the pair of genes at a given location (*locus*) on the *chromosome* map.

Amino acid One of a family of simple chemicals which number 20 in total. Assembled in chains, called *polypeptides*, amino acids are the basic units of *proteins*. The particular sequence of amino acids in any one protein is specified by a *gene*.

Amniocentesis The procedure by which a sample of amniotic fluid, which surrounds the developing foetus, is taken from the pregnant uterus.

Amniocytes The *cells* which are harvested from the amniotic fluid extracted by *amniocentesis*.

Amyloid precursor protein Metabolism of the substance called 'amyloid' is thought to be the central event in the causation of Alzheimer's disease, a neurodegenerative disorder characterised by premature senility. *Mutations* in the *gene* which codes for 'amyloid precursor protein' have been found in patients with Alzheimer's disease.

Aneuploidy The presence of an irregular number of *chromosomes* (which usually number 46 in humans). The most common type of aneuploidy is the gain or loss of one chromosome, eg. *trisomy* 21 (Down's syndrome).

Asymptomatic Not experiencing any symptoms of a particular disease or condition.

Autosomal Referring to, or determined by, a *gene* on a *chromosome* which is not sex determining (i.e. not X or Y).

Autosome Any of the *chromosomes* which are not sex determining (i.e, not the X or Y).

Base In genetics this refers to one of the four *nucleotides* (abbreviated to A, T, C and G) which are the components of *DNA*. Their sequence in a *gene* specifies both the *amino acids* and the sequence of amino acids in a *polypeptide*.

Base pair Referring to the *nucleotide bases*, 'A' and 'T', and 'C' and 'G', always link together and join the two strands of *DNA*.

Carcinogen A substance that provokes or encourages the onset or growth of cancer.

Carrier A healthy individual in whom one of a pair of *genes* is faulty or mutated.

Carrier detection A strategy, usually a biochemical or gene test, to identify individual(s) in whom one of a particular *gene* pair is faulty or mutated.

Carrier status The knowledge that an individual either is, or is not, the carrier of a particular gene fault.

Cationic liposome A chemical shell, composed of fat (lipid). In *gene therapy* it is hoped they might function as transporters of gene(s) to the tissue requiring genetic modification.

Cell The smallest unit of living organisms, which usually contains a *nucleus*. The adult human has some 50 billion cells.

Chorionic villus sampling (CVS) The procedure whereby a sample of tissue is taken from the chorionic membrane (the edge of the early placenta [afterbirth]) of the embryo.

Chromosomal Pertaining to chromosomes.

Chromosomal deletion The loss of a piece of inheritance material from the complement of *chromosomes*, which might be visibly detectable under the microscope, or invisible (submicroscopic).

Chromosome(s) Rod-like structures, or bundles, which contain the *DNA*, and therefore the *genes*, of a *cell*. Their structure is apparent when a cell divides to become two cells, otherwise they do not have a defined form and are visible under the microscope only as the *nucleus* of the cell. They are present in pairs, except in *gamete* cells (eggs and sperm).

Chromosome translocation The transfer and exchange of genetic material between different chromosomes which are not members of the same pair.

Chromosome disorder A genetic disease or *syndrome* due to an abnormal number or structure of chromosomes.

Clinical geneticist A physician who specialises in the diagnosis and management of hereditary diseases/disorders.

Cloning The process of isolating a specific *DNA* sequence or gene.

Codon Three consecutive *nucleotide bases* in *DNA* or *RNA* which specify an *amino acid*.

Concordance The degree to which both members of a twin pair show a particular *trait* or characteristic.

Congenital A defect or disease which is present from birth; this includes genetic and non-genetic conditions.

Consultand The individual (who may not be affected) through whom a family with a genetic disorder comes to be referred.

Correlation In scientific measurement, an expression of the closeness of relationship between two variables under study.

Creatine kinase A muscle *enzyme* which can be found in the blood. Increased levels are a general and non-specific indicator of muscle damage; it is an important investigation in sufferers (and *carriers*) of muscular dystrophy.

Culture A laboratory technique or process which facilitates the growth of tissues, cells or micro-organisms in an artificial environment.

Cytogenetics The study of *chromosomes* (as opposed to *genes*) – their structure, function and abnormalities.

Cytoplasm The substance of a *cell* within the boundaries of its membrane, excluding the *nucleus*.

Deletion Any loss of genetic material, which may therefore apply to a *chromosome* or *genes*.

Dinucleotide repeats A sequence of *DNA* in which two of the four *base pairs* alternate along its length.

Dizygotic (twins) Twins originating from two fertilised eggs.

DNA Deoxyribonucleic acid, the chemical of which *genes* are made, and which encodes genetic information.

DNA amplification The process of making many copies of a particular *DNA* sequence, by the technique of *PCR*.

DNA probing The technique of locating a *DNA* sequence of interest by using a complementary labelled strand of *DNA*.

Dominant A characteristic, disease, or disorder, which is manifest when only one member of the *gene* pair is altered, i.e. it is *expressed* in the *heterozygote*.

Electrophoresis See '*Gel electrophoresis*'.

Enzyme Any one of a large family of *proteins* produced by living organisms (the structure being encoded in a *gene*) which enhances, or catalyses, chemical or metabolic reactions in the body.

Eugenic The use of genetic measures to attempt to alter the genetic nature of a whole population.

Exon The region of a *gene* containing a coding sequence, and which is ultimately *expressed* in the formation of *messenger RNA* and *protein*. Most genes have several exons which are separated by *introns* which are usually longer.

Expression (of genetic information) The production by a *cell* of the *polypeptide* or *protein* for which the specific *gene* codes.

False negative A test result which has failed to detect the problem in an affected individual.

False positive A test result which is erroneously positive in an individual unaffected by the problem in question.

Family linkage study The use of DNA markers from members of a family for the purpose of establishing a genetic diagnosis in an individual. The same strategy can be used with big families to map a gene responsible for a particular condition.

Folic acid A vitamin, found ubiquitously in plants and animals, which has been shown to be important in reducing the incidence of neural tube defects (eg. spina bifida) when taken in adequate amounts by the mother around the time of conception.

Gamete The egg or sperm.

Gel electrophoresis In a genetics laboratory, the technique of separating different sized fragments of *DNA* or *RNA* by applying a directional electric current through a medium (the gel).

Gene The unit of inheritance, consisting of a sequence of *DNA* which codes for a specific *protein*, or part of a protein. Each *chromosome* contains hundreds, or possibly thousands, of *genes*.

Gene mapping The process of localising the position of *gene*s to their *chromosomal* site (*locus*).

Gene therapy Modification of the genetic make-up of the body *cells* of a patient in order to treat a disease.

Gene tracking The use of *genetic markers* to follow the inheritance of a *locus* in *cell* lines, family pedigrees or populations.

Genetic change See '*Mutation*'.

Genetic counselling The process whereby patients or relatives at risk of a disorder that may be hereditary are advised of the consequences of the disorder, the probability of developing and/or transmitting it, and of the ways in which this may be prevented or ameliorated. The approach is generally 'non-directive', thus allowing counsellees the opportunity of making their own informed decision(s).

Genetic engineering Any process which deliberately manipulates the make-up of the inheritance material of *cells*, tissues, or whole organisms.

Genetic marker An *allele*, or fragment of *DNA*, used in following the inheritance pattern of a *locus* (or loci) in *cell* lines, family pedigrees or populations.

Genetic testing Any investigation, for diagnostic or predictive purposes, which involves the analysis of fragments of *DNA*, either as part(s) of a *gene* or *linked* to a *locus* in question. Analysis of the *expression* of a gene, i.e. the *RNA*, is also included.

Genetics The scientific study of variation and heredity.

Genome The term variously used to describe the genetic complement of an individual, or of a particular species.

Genotype The genetic constitution of an individual, either in total or referring to a specific *locus*.

Germ line (cells) Those cells from which the *gametes* (eggs and sperm) are derived.

Guthrie test The screening test for phenylketonuria and congenital hypothyroidism performed on a drop of blood usually taken from the heel of newborn babies.

Heritability The proportion of variance of a characteristic which is due to genetic rather than environmental factors.

Heterogeneous In genetics, the occurrence of a single disease entity, or *phenotype*, due to *mutation* of more than one *gene*, which usually implies more than one genetic *locus*.

Heterozygote An individual who has inherited unlike *alleles* of a specific *gene* pair from the parents.

Heterozygote carrier See *'Carrier'*.

Histology The study of the minute structure of tissues using a microscope.

Homologous units Matched inheritance material, usually referring to the other member of a pair of *chromosomes* (or part thereof).

Homozygote An individual who has inherited identical *alleles* of a specific *gene* pair from the parents.

Human Genome Project The world wide collaborative effort to construct a genetic map of all the chromosomes and then establish the sequence of *nucleotide bases* which are thought to number approximately 3 billion.

Index case The affected individual who brings the family to medical attention; synonymous with the terms *proband* and propositus.

Instability With reference to the *genome*, a segment of *DNA* which has tendency (intrinsic or extrinsic) to alter in its characteristics as a result of the process of *cell* division.

Intron The region of a *gene* which separates *exons* or coding sequences.

Karyotype The chromosome constitution of an individual as displayed by a preparation of dividing chromosomes observed under the microscope.

Linkage analysis See *'Family linkage study'*.

Linked DNA markers See *'Genetic marker'*.

Locus In genetics, the place on a *chromosome* which is occupied by a *gene*.

Malformation A fault in the primary development of an organ or tissue, and therefore present at birth.

Meiosis The process of cell division which leads to the formation of *gametes* (eggs or sperm), and therefore involves a halving of the *chromosome* number (one member of each pair).

Mendelian (genetics) Patterns of inheritance which conform to the system proposed originally by Gregor Mendel.

Messenger RNA The type of *RNA* which is formed on the *DNA* template (*transcription*) and then processed for the production of a specific *polypeptide* (*translation*).

Mitosis The process of cell division of *somatic*, or body, cells which leads to daughter cells containing the full *chromosome* number (both members of each pair).

Molecular genetics The study of *DNA*, *RNA* and *genes*, and the processes that involve these structures in *cell* biology.

Monozygotic (twins) Twins derived from a single fertilised egg.

Multifactorial Refers to the type of inheritance determined by many factors including both *genes* and environment.

Mutation A defect, change, or alteration in *DNA*, which has genetic consequences.

Mutation analysis Any technique which makes it possible to detect alterations in *DNA*.

Nucleotide (base) One of the four constituent chemicals of *DNA* or *RNA* which provide an 'alphabet', whereby a combination of three codes each *amino acid*. In DNA the four are: adenine (A), thymine (T), cytosine (C), and guanine (G); in RNA uracil (U) replaces thymine.

Nucleus The large, dark staining part of a *cell* where the *chromosomes* are located.

Oncogene(s) A group, or family, of *genes* which behave in a *dominant* manner to induce or maintain *cell* transformation, and are therefore important in the generation of cancer.

Pathology The study of the essential nature of disease due to structural and functional changes in tissues and organs.

Pedigree A diagrammatic representation of a family history.

Penetrance The proportion of individuals with a particular genetic constitution who manifest its effect(s).

Pericentromeric (region) Pertaining to that part of a *chromosome* which is near the centromere – the junction of the short and long arms.

Phenotype The visible expression of the action of a particular gene, which usually refers to the overall clinical features resulting from a genetic disorder.

Phenylalanine One of the 20 naturally occurring *amino acids*. Levels of this amino acid increase in the disorder 'phenylketonuria' due to an *enzyme* deficiency and this increase is toxic to the developing brain, causing mental retardation if untreated.

Polygenic Inheritance determined by many *genes* at different *loci*, each with small additive effects, eg. height.

Polymer A large (macro) molecule composed of a number of repeat subunits (monomers) bonded together.

Polymerase chain reaction (PCR) The technique of amplification of short strands of *DNA*, which allows analysis of minute amounts of original DNA.

Polymorphism Frequent hereditary variations in *DNA* structure, i.e. sequence of *bases*, at a genetic *locus*.

Polypeptide The chain of *amino acids* which forms all or part of a *protein*.

Predictive testing The use of a genetic, or other, investigation which makes it possible to determine the genetic status of an individual before the onset of any clinical symptoms or signs related to the disorder in question.

Premutation A clinically insignificant change in a *gene* which predisposes to subsequent full *mutation* and clinical effects.

Prenatal testing The use of a genetic, biochemical, or other (eg. ultrasound scanning) investigation to make a diagnosis in the foetus.

Presymptomatic testing See '*Predictive testing*'.

Primers Short lengths of synthetic *DNA* which target the region of interest in the *genome*, so enabling the *polymerase chain reaction (PCR)* to take place.

Proband The affected individual who brings the family to medical attention; synonymous with the terms *index case* and propositus.

Probe A fragment of *DNA* which is labelled (often radioactively) and used to identify a complementary sequence.

Protein The complex structure made from one or more *polypeptide* chains.

Proto-oncogene A *gene* which has a role in normal *cell* growth and proliferation but when *mutated* may function as an *oncogene*.

Recessive A characteristic, disease, or disorder, which is manifest only when both members of a *gene* pair are altered, i.e. it is *expressed* in the *homozygote*.

Replication The process whereby *DNA* makes copies of itself when a *cell* divides.

Restriction enzyme(s) The group *proteins* which have the property of cutting the *DNA* chain at specific recognition sites.

Retrovirus Viruses are tiny infectious organisms which reproduce inside host *cells* and contain either *DNA* or *RNA* as their *genome*. Retroviruses contain RNA and when they infect cells their RNA genomes are converted to a DNA form which is then integrated into the host genome, where it replicates with each cell division.

RFLP – Restriction fragment length polymorphism Inherited variations in *DNA* length detected by cutting the DNA with a particular *restriction enzyme*.

Ribosome An intracellular structure which facilitates the process of *translation*.

RNA Ribonucleic acid. Forms of nucleic acid which are concerned with the synthesis of *protein*. See *'Messenger RNA'*, *'Transfer RNA'*, *'Transcription'* and *'Translation'*.

Screening The systematic application of a test or enquiry with the purpose of identifying individuals from a defined population who are either affected or at risk of a specific disorder, usually in order that a medical intervention can be instituted or offered.

Sensitivity An expression of the degree to which a particular test can detect the problem being looked for.

Sex chromosome The *chromosomes* which primarily govern sex determination

— XX in females, XY in males.

Sex-linked A term often used interchangeably with *X-linked* but strictly speaking refers to the inheritance of a gene or either of the sex-determining *chromosomes* (X and Y).

Single gene disorder A disease or condition due to damage (*mutation*) in one *gene*. The term does not distinguish between *dominant* or *recessive* inheritance.

Somatic Pertaining to the body *cells* as opposed to those of the *germ line*.

Southern analysis/blotting The technique whereby *DNA* is transferred to a backing sheet prior to *probing* (developed by Edward Southern in 1975).

Specificity A measure of the proportion of individuals with a positive *screening* test who do not have the problem being looked for. See *'False negative'* and *'False positive'*.

Syndrome A particular set of anomalies or features which are observed to occur repeatedly and in a consistently recognisable pattern.

Targeted screening The rational application of *screening* to (a) high risk group(s).

Teratogenic Describing a chemical, or other agent, which affects the developing foetus in such a way as to cause a *congenital malformation*.

Trait A characteristic, or feature for which a *gene* is responsible.

Transcription The production of *messenger RNA* from the *DNA* template.

Transfer RNA(s) Forms of *RNA* which recognise sets of three *nucleotides bases* (*codons*) in *messenger RNA* and transport specific *amino acids* for incorporation into a *polypeptide* chain.

Transgenic Describing the introduction of synthetic *DNA* into the *genome* of an animal in order to change its *genotype*.

Translation The conversion of the *messenger RNA* message to a *polypeptide* chain, which involves *ribosomes* and *transfer RNA*.

Transmission The passing of inheritance material or *alleles* from one generation to another.

Trinucleotide repeat A segment of *DNA* in which a triplet of *nucleotide bases* is repeated sequentially.

Triple test The antenatal *screening* test which combines the results of two tests on the mother's blood with her age to calculate the probability that the foetus has Down's *syndrome* (*trisomy* 21).

Trisomy The presence of three copies of a particular *chromosome*.

Tumour An abnormal new growth of *cells* in the body which continues after the cessation of the stimuli which have initiated it.

Tumour suppressor gene A *gene* which, when functioning normally, acts to pevent *cell* growth getting out of control. Loss of both copies of these genes in a cell, or tissue, usually results in *tumour* development and they therefore behave in a *recessive* manner at cell level.

Unstable mutation See *'Instability'*.

Variable expression The difference in manifestations or severity of a particular genetic disorder between affected members of the same family.

X-linked Refers to *genes* carried on the X *chromosome*, a disease due to *mutation* in such a gene, or the pattern of inheritance of such a disease.

Zygote The fertilised egg.

Further reading

Books

A Practical Guide to Human Cancer Genetics, S V Hodgson and E R Maher, Cambridge University Press, 1993.

Children in Care – The medical contribution, BAAF, 1989.

Children of Incest: Whose secret is it?, Alexina McWhinnie and Daphne Batty, BAAF, 1993.

Effectiveness and efficiency: random reflections on health care services, A L Cochrane, BMJ and The Nuffield Provincial Hospitals Trust, Cambridge University Press, 1989.

Essential Medical Genetics (4th edn), J M Connor and M A Ferguson-Smith, Blackwell Scientific Publications, 1993.

Genetic Counselling: Its practice and principles, (ed.) A Clarke, Routledge, 1994.

Genetics in Medicine, M W Thompson, R R McInnes, and H F Willard, W B Saunders, 1991.

Genome, Jerry E. Bishop & Michael Waldholz, Simon & Schuster, 1990, USA.

Human Genetic Information, Ciba Foundation Symposium 149, John Wiley & Sons, 1990.

Medical Ethics Today: Its practice and philosophy, British Medical Association's Ethics, Science and Information Division, BMJ Publishing Group, 1993.

Molecular Genetics for the Clinician, D J H Brock, Cambridge University Press, 1993.

Our Genetic Future: The science and ethics of genetic technology, BMA, Oxford University Press, 1992.

Practical Genetic Counselling, Peter Harper, Butterworth-Heinemann Ltd, 1993.

Prenatal diagnosis and screening, (eds) D J H Brock, C H Rodeck, M A Ferguson-Smith, Churchill Livingstone, 1992.

Prenatal Diagnosis: The human side, (eds) L Abramsky and J Chapple, Chapman and Hall, 1994.

The Genetic Revolution, (ed.) Bernard D Davis, The Johns Hopkins University Press, 1991, USA.

The haemoglobinopathies in Europe – a report of the first two meetings of the WHO European/Mediterranean Working Group on haemoglobinopathies, EUR/ICP/MCH 110 3370, World Health Organisation, Geneva.

The Language of the Genes, Steve Jones, HarperCollins, 1993.

The Lottery of Life, Philippe Frossard, Bantam Press, 1991.

The New Genetics and Clinical Medicine, (3rd edn) D J Weatherall, Oxford University Press, 1991.

Wonderwoman and Superman, John Harris, Oxford University Press, 1992.

Articles

'A novel gene containing a trinucleotide repeat that is expanded and unstable on Huntington's disease chromosomes', The Huntington's Disease Collaborative Research Group, *Cell*, 72:971-983, 1993.

'Cloning of the essential myotonic dystrophy region and mapping of the putative defect', C Aslanidis, G Jansen, C Amemiya, et al, *Nature*, 355:548-551, 1992.

'Complete cloning of the Duchenne muscular dystrophy (DMD) cDNA and preliminary genomic organization of the DMD gene in normal and affected individuals' by M Koenig, E P Hoffman, C J Bertelson, et al, *Cell*, 50:509-517, 1987.

'Cystic fibrosis carrier screening', Z H Miedzybrodzka, *Journal SOGC*, 135-143, 1993.

'Diagnosis of genetic disorders at the DNA level', by S E Antonarakis, *New England Journal of Medicine*, 320:153-163, 1989, USA.

'Identification of a gene (FMR-1) containing a CGG repeat coincident with a breakpoint cluster region exhibiting length variation in Fragile X syndrome', A J M H Verkerk, M Pieretti, J S Sutcliffe, et al, *Cell*, 65:905-914, 1991.

214

'Identification of the cystic fibrosis gene; cloning and characterization of complementary DNA' by J R Riordan, J J Rommens, B S Kerem, et al, *Science* 245:1066-73, 1989.

'Molecular basis of myotonic dystrophy: expansion of a trinucleotide (CTG) repeat at the 3' end of transcript encoding a protein kinase family member', by J D Brook, M E McCurrach, H G Harley, et al, *Cell*, 68:799-808, 1992.

'The genetics of schizophrenia and its implications', A Holland, R Murray, and S Brandon, *Adoption and Fostering*, 9:2, 1985.

Regional genetic centres

East Anglia
Genetic Counselling Service
Addenbrooke's Hospital
Hills Road, Cambridge CB2 2QQ
01223 216446/217027

Merseyside
Regional Genetic Counselling Service
Paediatric Department
Countess of Chester Hospital
Liverpool Road, Chester CH2 2BA
01244 365061

Regional Genetic Counselling Service
Royal Liverpool Hospital
PO Box 147
Liverpool L69 3BX
0151 706 4019

Northern
Department of Human Genetics
University of Newcastle
19 Claremont Place
Newcastle upon Tyne NE1 4LP
0191 2325131

North Western
Department of Medical Genetics
St Mary's Hospital
Hathersage Road
Manchester M13 0JH
0161 276 1234

Department of Clinical Genetics
Royal Manchester Children's Hospital
Pendlebury
Manchester M27 1HA
0161 794 4696 ex. 2335

Oxford
Department of Medical Genetics
Churchill Hospital
Old Road, Headington
Oxford OX3 7LD
01865 741841

South Western
Regional Cytogenetics Services
Southmead Hospital
Bristol BS10 5NB
0117 9505050

Clinical Genetics Department
Royal Hospital for Sick Children
St Michael's Hill
Bristol BS5 5BJ
0117 9215411

Clinical Genetics Service
Department of Child Health
Royal Devon & Exeter Hospital
(Wonford)
Barrack Road
Exeter EX2 5DW
01392 403151

Thames Region

North East Thames
Clinical Genetics Unit
Institute of Child Health
30 Guildford Street
London WC1N 1EA
0171 242 9789

Clinical Genetics Unit
Royal Free Hospital
Pond Street
London NW3 2QG
0171 794 0500 ex. 5163

North West Thames
Kennedy Galton Centre for Clinical
Genetics
Northwick Park Hospital
Harrow, Middx HA1 3UJ
0181 422 8577

South East Thames
Paediatrics Research Unit
Guy's Hospital
London SE1 9RT
0171 955 4648

South West Thames
Regional Genetics Services
St George's Hospital
Cranmer Terrace
London SW17 0RE
0181 767 8150

Trent
Department of Clinical Genetics
Leicester Royal Infirmary
Leicester LE1 5WW
0116 2541414 ex. 5836

Department of Clinical Genetics
City Hospital
Hucknall Road
Nottingham NG5 1PB
0115 9627728

Centre for Human Genetics
117 Manchester Road
Sheffield S10 5DN
0114 2667333

Wessex
Regional Genetics Services
Princess Anne Hospital
Coxford Road
Southampton SO9 4HA
01703 796169

West Midlands
West Midlands Regional Genetics
Services
Birmingham Maternity Hospital
Edgbaston
Birmingham B15 2TH
0121 472 5199

Regional Genetics Services
East Birmingham Hospital
Bordesley Green East
Birmingham B9 5ST
0121 766 6611

Yorkshire
Department of Clinical Genetics
Ashley Wing
St James's Hospital
Leeds LS2 7TF
0113 2837070

Scotland

Regional Genetics Services
Ward 3-4
Aberdeen Royal Infirmary
Foresterhill
Aberdeen AB9 2ZA
01224 681818 ex. 52120

Regional Genetics Services
Department of Pathology
Ninewells Teaching Hospital
NHS Trust
Dundee DD1 9SY
01382 660111 ex. 2035

Department of Medicine
Human Genetics Unit
Western General Hospital
Crewe Road
Edinburgh EH4 2XU
0131 332 2525 ex. 4535

Duncan Guthrie Institute of Medical
Genetics
Royal Hospital for Sick Children
Yorkhill, Glasgow G3 8SJ
0141 339 8888 ex. 4365

Regional Genetics Services
Raigmore Hospital
Inverness IV2 3UJ
01463 234151 ex. 2310

Wales
Institute of Medical Genetics
University Hospital of Wales
Heath Park
Cardiff CF4 4XN
01222 747747

Northern Ireland
Department of Medical Genetics
Floor A, West Podium Extension
Tower Block, Belfast City Hospital
51 Lisburn Road
Belfast BT9 7AB
01232 329241 ex. 2323

Notes on contributors

Dr Angus Clarke

Dr Angus Clarke works as a Clinical Geneticist, seeing individuals and families with genetic disease for diagnosis, counselling and clinical management. He has worked as a Senior Lecturer in Cardiff for 6 years. His research interests include the social and ethical issues raised by the genetic testing of children.

Dr Deepthi de Silva

Dr Deepthi de Silva is a Senior Registrar in Clinical Genetics working in Aberdeen. She has a clinical and research interest in the counselling, screening and genetic testing of families with a cancer predisposition and the repercussions of such intervention to individuals identified as being at risk.

Dr John C S Dean

Dr John Dean trained at Cambridge and Edinburgh Universities and has been a Consultant in Clinical Genetics in Aberdeen since 1990. He has a special interest in hereditary heart disorders and has undertaken research in Marfan syndrome, the Long QT syndromes and CATCH22.

Donal Giltinan

Donal Giltinan is a Social Work Manager and a Consultant Trainer at the Scottish Centre of British Agencies for Adoption & Fostering. Since 1975 he has been closely involved in the placement of older children for adoption; recruiting and preparing families, supporting families after placement, and providing training and consultancy to the panels of people who consider adoption and fostering applications. With Susan Macleod, he is co-author of a modest book *Child Care Law: A summary of the law in Scotland* and has contributed to several articles in medical, legal and social work journals.

Dr Anne Grant

Dr Anne Grant is a Senior Medical Officer in Community Child Health with Edinburgh Sick Children's NHS Trust, and has been an Adoption Medical Adviser since 1985. During this period, she has had a particular interest in reviewing the medical, developmental and psychological profiles of children being placed in long-term permanent substitute care, and is currently part of a working group in Lothian looking at medical assessment and supervision of children in care.

Dr Neva Haites

Dr Neva Haites obtained a PhD in Biochemistry in Australia and on moving to Scotland studied and obtained medical qualifications in Aberdeen, where she then went on to train as a Clinical Geneticist. She is currently a Reader in Medical Genetics in the University of Aberdeen and Head of Service in Medical Genetics at the Aberdeen Royal Hospitals NHS Trust. Her research and clinical interests include inherited predisposition to cancers, peripheral neuropathy and retinal degeneration.

Dr Margaret A Irving

Dr Margaret A Irving has been the Lead Clinician, Child and Family Health, Dumfries and Galloway Community Unit, since April 1994. She has also been the Medical Adviser to the Adoption and Fostering Panel for 10 years. She is past Chair of the Scottish Medical General BAAF Committee 1990-93 and is a current member of the BAAF Scottish Medical Group.

Dr K F Kelly

Dr K F Kelly gained a BSc in Biochemistry followed by a PhD in Physiology. He then spent two years in the Department of Molecular Biology (University of Edinburgh) and three years at the University of Liverpool. He has been in charge of the Molecular Genetics Diagnostic Laboratory in Aberdeen since 1986.

Dr Theresa Marteau

Dr Theresa Marteau is Director of the Psychology and Genetics Research Group at United Medical and Dental Schools of Guy's and St. Thomas's in London. Her current research into the psychological and social consequences of the new human genetics focuses upon perceptions of risk and doctor-patient communication.

Dr Susan Michie

Dr Susan Michie is Research Fellow at the Psychology and Genetics Research Group in London. After qualifying as a clinical psychologist, she did a doctorate in developmental psychology. She has used this clinical and research background in conducting health services research, including the evaluation of genetic counselling.

Dr Zofia Miedzybrodzka

Dr Zofia Miedzybrodzka is a Clinician with a background in both obstetrics and genetics. She is interested in the clinical, psychological, laboratory and economic aspects of population genetic screening programmes, and has performed a series of studies of cystic fibrosis carrier screening.

Marjorie Morrison

Marjorie Morrison is a Child Placement Consultant at BAAF. Having started an interest in adoption through the placement of babies in a local authority setting, she has now specialised in this area for over 20 years. Much of this time has involved the complexities of linking children with special needs with substitute families which sometimes raises particular genetic concerns and always requires an understanding of the long-term implications of genealogical discontinuity.

Dr Michael Morton

Dr Michael Morton is Consultant Child Psychiatrist at Ladyfield, Dumfries and a member of the Executive of the Scottish Medical Group of BAAF. His interest in adoption arises from practice within Dumfries and Galloway and in the In-Patient Unit which offers assessment and treatment for children from a wider area.

Dr Heather Payne

Dr Heather Payne has been Medical Adviser to South Glamorgan Adoption Agency since 1990, and is Divisional Medical Adviser to Barnardo's South Wales and South West. She is currently Chair of the BAAF Welsh Medical Group and a member of the National BAAF Medical Executive Committee. She is also associated with The British Association for Community Child Health Wales and After Adoption Wales. Her research interests are currently on outcomes in adoption including evaluation of post-adoption services, and health status of looked after children.

Alexandra Plumtree

Alexandra Plumtree is the Scottish Legal Consultant for BAAF. She qualified as a solicitor in Scotland in 1977, and has worked since then in private practice, and as a Reporter to the Children's Panel. She has extensive experience of the public and private law of the family and children in Scotland.

Professor J A Raeburn

Professor J A Raeburn is a Professor of Clinical Genetics at Nottingham

University and Clinical Director of the Genetic Services; he has a special interest in genetics in the community. His special interest is in genetic counselling, especially for conditions such as the Fragile X syndrome, cystic fibrosis and Huntington's disease.

Dr Sheila A Simpson

Dr Sheila Simpson is a Clinical Geneticist with a special interest in neurogenetics, and the problems of counselling for predictive testing for adult onset diseases. The use and abuse of genetic information, especially with regard to adoption, are a continuing clinical and research interest.

Dr Peter Turnpenny

Dr Peter Turnpenny is Consultant Clinical Geneticist at the Royal Devon and Exeter Healthcare NHS Trust, Exeter. He graduated from Edinburgh University Medical School. After a variety of hospital jobs, culminating in paediatric registrar training at Aberdeen, he worked at the Nazareth Hospital (Edinburgh Medical Missionary Society), Israel, from 1983-90 as head of paediatrics, during which time his interest in clinical genetics developed. On returning to the UK he took up formal training at Aberdeen and served on the Committee of the Scottish section of the BAAF Medical Group. Since October 1993 he has been a Consultant at Exeter providing the Clinical Genetics Service for Devon and Cornwall.

Index

personality *1, 9, 94, 98*

phenylketonuria (PKU) *86, 101, 128, 156, 159*

Pick disease *96*

porphyria *101-2*

predictive testing *96, 117, 122, 150, 170-2, 176-9, 181, 185, 197, 200*

presymptomatic testing *80, 130, 156*

pregnancy *43, 46, 54, 59-60, 101, 103, 157-61, 166, 173*

psychiatric disorders *15-6, 63, 94-5, 97-8*

psychological identity *166*

R

race and heredity *13*

racism *13*

recessive inheritance (see also *autosomal recessive*) *28*

RNA *83-4*

S

schizophrenia *30, 36, 38, 61, 63-4, 97-8, 181*

screening *5, 6, 37, 110, 117-9, 134, 153, 155-60, 162-4, 182-3, 195, 197*

sex-linked disorders *77*

single gene disorders *72-3, 77, 80, 83, 145-6*

social work *21-2, 24, 40, 52, 201*

social worker(s) *5-6, 9, 11, 13, 18, 21, 24, 27, 30, 40-1, 45, 51, 53, 184, 188, 191*

Southern analysis *87-9, 92*

T

Tay-Sachs disease *13, 158, 162-3*

thalassaemia *12, 157, 159*

Tourette syndrome *100*

trinucleotide repeats *88, 90-1*

tuberous sclerosis *36, 38*

W

Williams syndrome *127*

X

X-linked *13, 98, 142*
chromosome *90, 103-4*
gene *51*
inheritance *98*

XYY syndrome *99*

Y

Y chromosome *99*